Hunters in the Barrens

Hunters in the Barrens

The Naskapi
on the Edge of the White Man's World

Georg Henriksen

Berghahn Books

New York • Oxford

Published in 2010 by
Berghahn Books
www.berghahnbooks.com

©2010 Institute of Social and Economic Research

Originally published by the Institute of Social and Economic Research,
Memorial University of Newfoundland.

Library of Congress Cataloging-in-Publication Data

Henriksen, Georg.
   Hunters in the barrens : the Naskapi on the edge of the white man's
world / Georg Henriksen.
   p. cm.
   Includes bibliographical references and index.
   ISBN 978-1-84545-950-5
  1. Naskapi Indians–Hunting. 2. Naskapi Indians–Migrations. 3.
Naskapi Indians–Social life and customs. 4. Davis Strait–Social life and
customs. 5. Labrador (N.L.)–Social life and customs. I. Title.
E99.N18H46 2010
971.8'201--dc22   2010027184

British Library Cataloguing in Publication Data

A catalogue record for this book is available from the British Library

Printed in the United States on acid-free paper.

ISBN: 978-1-84545-950-5 (paperback)

Contents

List of Maps, Figures and Tables

Foreword

Georg Henriksen's *Hunters in the Barrens* has become a classic: between 1973 and 1997 the Institute of Social and Economic Research published seventeen reprints – and requests for the book will, I am sure, continue unabated with its new publisher, Berghahn Books. In the 1973 Foreword I wrote that for future generations of Innu (Naskapi)[1] this book would be an important legacy. So it has come to be, and the late Georg Henriksen himself further ensured it with the publication of his biography of an Innu friend, *I Dreamed the Animals: Kaniuekutat, The Life of an Innu Hunter* (Berghahn, 2009). Speaking of legacies, Georg himself is an anthropological legacy: right up to his last days (he died in 2007) he remained in touch with the Innu with whom he first lived in 1966. For Georg, life as an anthropologist – and the responsibilities thereof – went far beyond writing a thesis and securing a university appointment. In his work with government committees concerning the Labrador Innu, he helped to focus attention on problems facing the Innu along with suggestions for their solution or at least amelioration.

Of course much about the life of the Innu has changed since Georg first knew them, and I invite the reader to turn to the Afterword by Peter Armitage, a colleague of Georg's, for a responsible account of those changes and Georg's part in them.

Robert Paine,†
Professor Emeritus,
Memorial University of Newfoundland

---

1. The Labrador Innu with whom Georg worked, and who were formerly referred to as Naskapi, refer to themselves nowadays as Mushuau Innu (or Mushuaunnuat in standard orthography).

Preface

This study is the result of two separate visits, one while I was a research fellow with the Institute of Social and Economic Research, Memorial University, and the other while I was a research associate in the ISER project *Identity and Modernity in the East Arctic* sponsored by the Izaak Walton Killam Awards. The material was collected in the periods June 1966 to June 1967, and December 1967 to June 1968, respectively.

Of the many persons drawn into this study, my warmest thanks go first and foremost to the Naskapi in Davis Inlet who accepted my intrusion into their society. Special thanks are due to Thomas and Alice Noa who, from the beginning, received me into their tent, and eased the period of accommodation both for me and the Naskapi. Special thanks are also due to Sam and Shibish Napeo who came to be my best friends while I was a member of their household in the Barren Grounds. It was Napeo who taught me how to become a Naskapi man, so that I could participate as a hunter in their ritual of *mokoshan*.

I am also grateful to the missionary and the storekeeper and his wife in Davis Inlet. I am painfully aware of the fact that this study does not do justice to the work of these two men in Davis Inlet. Alone, the missionary stood up on behalf of the Naskapi and protected their rights to their land and their rights to remain in Davis Inlet as long as they chose. In these and many other matters concerning Davis Inlet, we are in full agreement.

I wish to thank all those who have given me valuable suggestions at various stages of my work with the material; in particular, to Professors Robert Paine, Fredrik Barth, and Jean Briggs who read various versions of the manuscript and gave me detailed criticism. I also wish to thank Cato Wadel, Jan-Petter Blom, and Otto Blehr for the stimulating and encouraging discussions I have had with them. Thanks also to Professors Edward Rogers, David Alexander, and George Park who read the manuscript on my request. Finally, I wish to thank Sonia Kuryliw Paine for her editorial work and the secretaries at Memorial University and the University of Bergen for typing the various versions of the manuscript.

February, 1973

Georg Henriksen
Bergen, Norway

Introduction

The Naskapi live in two different worlds: in the winter, they roam the interior of Labrador, hunting caribou; in the summer, they live in or around the village of Davis Inlet on the coast of Labrador. In this book, one of the themes I explore is the contrast in the social life between these two worlds. One may say that the Naskapi alternate between two economic spheres: the subsistence sphere of caribou hunting in the winter, and the money sphere of cod fishing in the summer. However, their lives are altered not only in economic terms, but also ecologically, socially, and ideologically, so that one may say that the Naskapi alternate between two life spheres.

In Sango Bay, approximately ten miles from Davis Inlet, lives an isolated settler family that exploits the same environment as the Naskapi. Yet, the only son is able to earn $6,000 a year, while a Naskapi seldom makes more than $1,500. This great difference in income is readily, though superficially explained if we look at the yearly round of activities of the settler and the Naskapi. However, the question remains: why do the Naskapi not exploit the environment in the same manner as the settler does? While the settler lives in his house by the sea year-round earning money by fishing and sealing, the Naskapi leave the coast in the fall to go hunting caribou in the Barren Grounds throughout the winter. Their life here earns them little or no cash, is very strenuous and implies a certain risk through sickness and starvation. Why do they prefer it to the safe and comfortable life on the coast where they could earn more cash and buy more material goods, both of which they value, or simply live off relief?

From the preceding remarks, it can be seen that the two worlds offer very different opportunities for the Naskapi, and I shall try to analyse some of the crucial values which they share and pursue in the two situations. It is not a question of the Naskapi having two different sets of values, one belonging to the coastal world, and another to the Barren Ground world. Rather, as I shall demonstrate, the Naskapi hold the same values in both worlds, but the opportunities to maximize these values differ in the two worlds. As a consequence of this fact, the quality of life differs radically, as does the relative richness of meaning which the two worlds represent to the Naskapi.

I shall argue that the harsh environment of the interior provides a setting for joint activities through which shared values are consummated. The focal point for these activities and the one foremost in the minds of the Naskapi is the caribou. The Naskapi pursue herds of caribou as they feed widely scattered on the semi-barren plateau in the interior of Labrador. In tents made out of flimsy cotton duck, the hunters and their families subsist on caribou throughout the arctic winter. The caribou, the caribou hunt, and the sharing of its produce lie at the heart of Naskapi culture. The sacred marrow from the long bones of the caribou is eaten raw by all the hunters in a ritual context where crucial cultural values are communicated and confirmed. Inside one tent, they sit in a circle for a whole day, partaking in this communal meal through which their relationship to the natural and supernatural worlds is expressed. Also communicated in the ritual are some of the dominant characteristics of their social life, notably that of the fundamental interdependence of one Naskapi upon the other, and the importance of sharing the fruits of the hunt. The environment of the Barren Ground world makes them dependent upon one another.

Yet, simultaneously with this interdependence, I shall argue that individual autonomy is also a central value for the Naskapi. Their adaptation as hunters makes it possible for them to attain an exceptionally high degree of autonomy. Thus, the Naskapi are confronted with a fundamental dilemma: on the one hand, the harsh environment forces dependence upon each other, while on the other, they wish to maximize their autonomy and personal individuality.

In the course of my analysis, I shall discuss another basic dilemma in the Naskapi culture: that of sharing versus having. Sharing, especially that of caribou meat, is fundamental to the social system of the Naskapi. It is with the knowledge that successful hunters will share their kill with the others, that most of the Naskapi are able to travel into the Barren Grounds with their families. Also, through sharing a hunter can gain a following and prestige. But, at the same time, the individual Naskapi also values having and keeping for himself. Hence, sharing is encumbered with many sanctions; keeping anything that should be shared makes one a target for social contempt.

We shall see that the Naskapi manage to cope with these dilemmas in the Barren Ground world, but they become more acute in the coastal world, and have different behavioural consequences. This is so because of the different opportunities presented in the coastal and interior worlds. On the coast, new and non-traditional transformations of economic goods are possible and desirable, whereas crucial traditional values and goals are difficult or impossible to realize in this ecological setting. While the core of their culture belongs to the Barren Grounds, the Naskapi, nevertheless, value the safety and comfort of living on the coast, in touch with the white man's world. However, problems exist because they have not adapted efficiently to the market economy.

On the coast, it is possible to exercise autonomy to an extent never attainable in the interior. At the same time, it is also possible to maximize the value of having, and neglect the traditional rules of sharing. Thus, the two dilemmas in the value system of the Naskapi come to a head on the coast, and this leads to open interpersonal conflicts. I shall argue that the perpetual quarrelling and heavy drinking, so characteristic of social life on the coast, is due largely to the discrepancy between Naskapi values and goals and the opportunities they have for their realization in the two different settings. The disruptive effects on social life on the coast are caused by the lack of opportunities to act out traditional role behaviour with respect to being a hunter, a leader, and husband. The new opportunities and constraints regarding the allocation of economic goods necessitate making choices which are inconsistent with traditional ideas concerning the circulation of goods.

Although one may say that the Naskapi have become acculturated in the sense that they have adopted, and have grown dependent upon goods from the industrial world outside, the superficiality of their effects on Naskapi culture should emerge throughout this book. The Naskapi are still hunters at heart.

Note

The orthography used in the present text for Mushuau Innu (Naskapi) words is a convention adopted in the field. Note particularly that the "o" ought to be substituted with /u/. For recent linguistic transcription see Lynn Drapeau and José Mailhot, 1989, *Guide pratique d'orthographe montagnaise*. Québec: Institut éducatif et culturel attikamek-montagnais (English translation by Marguerite MacKenzie, Department of Linguistics, Memorial University of Newfoundland, 1991). http://www.innu-aimun.ca/modules/spelling/files/Guide_Montagnais_Spelling.pdf

Part I: The Setting

The Naskapi and their Environment

1

The hunting grounds of the Naskapi lie roughly within a semi-ellipse, reckoning 150 miles west and 50 miles north and south of Davis Inlet. It is the interior western part of this area where the Naskapi hunt for caribou which provides the setting for the most crucial aspects of Naskapi social life and culture. Their environment consists mainly of barren mountains and rolling plains broken up by numerous lakes and rivers. Throughout this exposed landscape, widely scattered patches of conifers are found in protected riverbeds and on a few sheltered hillsides. Here the Naskapi erect their tents, while the daily hunting activities take place in the surrounding wind-swept Barren Grounds. When on the move, the Naskapi travel swiftly from one stand of forest to the next, as they are dependent upon trees for the construction of their tents and wood for their stoves.

The Naskapi spend the best part of the winter, from October/December to March/April, in this part of Labrador. While the summers are often warmer in the interior than on the coast, the winters are always colder with temperatures dropping to –40°C and –50°C. The air is very dry, so that the climate can be characterized as arctic (Tanner, 1944:329). Ice begins to form on the lakes by the middle of September, and all smaller lakes are iced over by the beginning of October. By November/December, the rivers are frozen and safe for travel by dog-sled. The snow lies relatively deep in the woods and on the rivers, making travelling back and forth from the interior a strenuous task. But on the Barren Grounds, the snow is blown away so that usually one can walk without snowshoes. Lichen often lies exposed, making it easy for the caribou to feed.

Today the caribou hunt takes place mainly in the winter when the caribou are found feeding on the Barren Grounds. However, under special circumstances, it may happen that big herds migrate to the coast and even venture out to the islands. This occurred in the winter of 1965/66 presumably because mild weather and subsequent frost caused a layer of ice to form over the lichen, forcing the caribou out of the interior. The Naskapi reckon that certain parts of their hunting

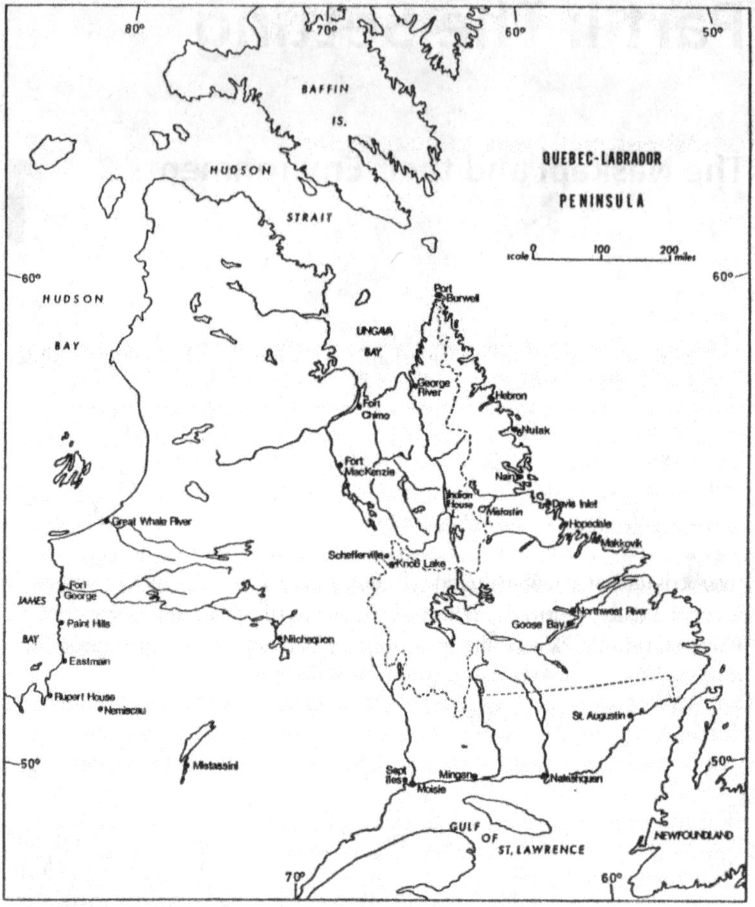

Map 1. Quebec-Labrador Peninsula

grounds always contain "plenty of caribou." One area is particularly favoured where, the Naskapi maintain, "the caribou cannot get out." They say they can shoot for a whole day, and still, caribou return a day or two later.

Some Naskapi make short hunting trips during the summer when the caribou often feed close to the coast. It is only the late summer skin that can be used for fur coats, as the winter skin sheds rapidly.

Of the various other land mammals hunted in winter, the porcupine is highly valued for its palatable skin, fat, and meat. It is found in the woods only, so that the Naskapi catch it mostly while travelling to or from the interior. Wolves abound also, but they are difficult and time-consuming to hunt or trap, so that the Naskapi get only a few each year. Arctic fox (white and blue) and red fox (cross between black and brown) are numerous, but are not hunted or trapped systematically. Otter and lynx are hunted in the woods if the opportunity arises and a few are caught each year. All the above animals are valued for their fur and meat. Mink and weasel are trapped for their fur only, but are eaten in times of scarcity when the Naskapi will also hunt hares and squirrels. The Naskapi say that they would never eat mice and lemming.

A frequent addition to the diet is the rock-ptarmigan. This bird is abundant everywhere in the hunting grounds of the Naskapi. Also important is the spruce partridge which is shot year-round although it is found only in the woods. Another welcome addition to the diet is red char which is caught now and then through the ice on the lakes.

Sometime during March or April, the Naskapi start their trek towards Davis Inlet. As they move eastward, the rolling barren plains become more mountainous so that they must follow the rivers which cut through coniferous forests and which eventually drain into the sea. The forest becomes more dense in the river valleys approximately thirty miles from the coast.

Finally, the Naskapi reach salt water in one of the numerous bays that indent the coastline at a stretch of ten to twenty miles from the sea. Along with the bays, hundreds of islands fringe this coastal part of the hunting grounds (see Map 2). The outer islands lie barren and exposed to the Atlantic Ocean, but nearer the mainland, they become heavily wooded and separated from each other and from the mainland by narrow sounds, rattles, and bays. The Naskapi feel more at ease among the inner islands and in the bays, the outer islands being quite hazardous for travellers in both summer and winter. In summer, the boats must be piloted between low skerries and sunken rocks, while in winter, the hunter must avoid areas where strong tidal currents prevent the water from freezing to form a safe layer of ice. Another danger exists in moving ice which can leave the hunter and his dog team on an isolated ice floe. Moving ice can also trap a small boat in late spring and early summer, especially in narrow sounds where it can quickly jam as it moves back and forth with the tidal current.

Although the sea ice starts to break up sometime in May, it is usually not gone before the beginning of July. By then it is summer on land, with temperatures of +30°C not being uncommon in Davis Inlet. However, snowfall can occur in July, caused by easterly winds that sweep in from the Atlantic and the Labrador Current, bringing cold weather with fog and rain to the coast. During August, the weather becomes rapidly colder with ice beginning to form on the lakes in September. In the middle of December, the sea starts to freeze up and becomes safe for travel except through rattles where strong tidal currents prevent ice from forming. The sea freezes way out from the shore, and the sparsely populated coast lies white, silent, and desolate under the northern lights.

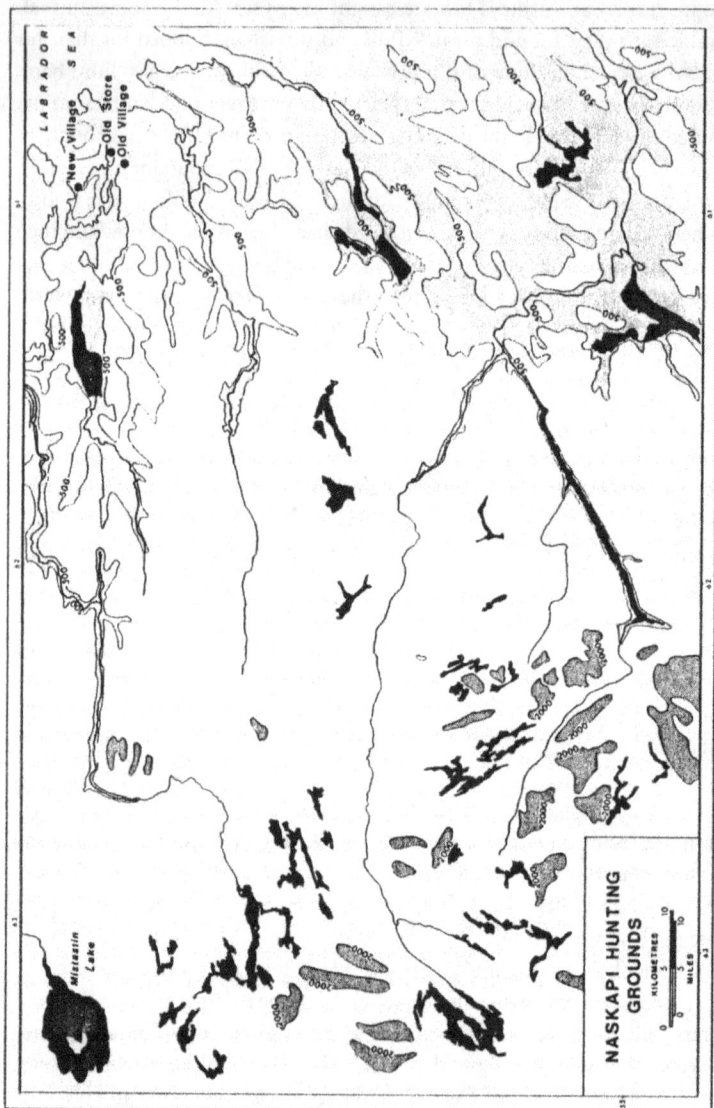

Map 2. Naskapi Hunting Grounds

When the Naskapi reach the coast and Davis Inlet in March/April, the weather can be warm and the seals are found basking on the ice in the sun. Throughout their stay on the coast, the Naskapi hunt for seals, the most common in the area being the harp seal and the jar seal; occasionally a square flipper is shot. The seal meat (and fat) is the most popular dog food, and although the Naskapi also eat it, they prefer other kinds of meat. The sealskin is used for boots, moccasins, and sled-lashes; only seldom is it sold to the store.

The Naskapi spend most of their time in the community, although most of them occasionally set up camps where they can utilize resources not found in the immediate surroundings of Davis Inlet. For example, in the spring they move into the bays to fish brook and lake trout through the ice on the lakes. They also hunt for black bear when it comes out of hibernation. At the end of May, the Canada goose arrives and large flocks can be found in open rattles in the bays. Later, they take to their nesting areas in the marshes close to the coast. In addition to the rock ptarmigan and the spruce partridge, the Naskapi also hunt black duck, eider duck, the loon, and the sea pigeon.

In July, cod fish reach the Labrador coast in large numbers, and constitute the main source of cash income for the Naskapi. Also abundant is the arctic char and less so, the atlantic salmon. Rock cod is important as a food resource. A small fish, the caplin, appears in great numbers for a short period in summer, spawning on sandy shores where it then dies. A few Naskapi collect it for dog food. Some of the older men used to dry the caplin and bring it into the interior as dog food, but nobody does so today.

Below is a chart (see p. 6) showing the seasonal exploitation of the various renewable resources upon which the Naskapi base their existence. In 1968, there were 145 Naskapi exploiting these various resources within a territory measuring roughly 15,000 square miles. In 1965, 45.7 of the population were fifteen years or younger (see figure 1). In 1968, there were 33 Naskapi households in Davis Inlet of which 2 did not travel into the Barren Grounds as the heads of these households were no longer active hunters. Among the 31 hunters, 2 were young men in their late teens who had not yet established their own households and therefore did little hunting.

Thus, the Naskapi are a small group of people who hunt in a vast tract of land with almost no competition from outside groups. The boundaries of their hunting territory are determined by the distance they wish and are able to travel. It is essential to realize that there are no families or other groups of people having rights to any of this territory or its resources. Every Naskapi is free to roam where he likes and exploit the resources of the land. Indeed, it would seem difficult to have any kind of family hunting territory system in a society where mobility is essential for exploiting migrating caribou herds.

Speck and Eiseley (1939, 1942), and Leacock (1954) recognize that this ecological adaptation militates against the possibility of any system of family

Table 1. Seasonal Exploitation of the Renewable Resources of the Naskapi

SEASON:	Autumn	Winter	Spring	Summer
PLACE OF CAMP:	**In the bays**	**Barren Lands**	**Davis Inlet/ In the bays**	**Davis Inlet**
RESOURCES EXPLOITED:				
caribou	sporad/ intens. many	intens. plenty	sporad/ intens. few	sporad. few
wolf	sporad. few	sporad. few	sporad. few	sporad. few
fox	sporad. few	sporad/intens. many	sporad. few	sporad. few
mink/ otter/ lynx	all sporad. few	all sporad. few	all sporad. few	all sporad. few
porcupine	intens. many	sporad/intens. few	sporad/intens. few	sporad. few
bear	sporad. few	none	sporad/intens. few	sporad. few
seal	intens. plenty	none	intens. plenty	sporad. many
Artic char/ salmon/cod/ rock-cod/	Arc. Char intens.	red char sporad.	Arc. Char/ rock-cod intens.	cod/ Arc.char/ salmon
red char	plenty	few	plenty	intens. plenty
geese/ducks/ ptarmigan	ptarmigan intens. sporad plenty	ptarmigan intens/ sporad. plenty	all intens. plenty	ducks/geese many

Hunted intensively: intens.
Hunted sporadically: sporad.
Number of specimens obtained: plenty, many, few.

```
                    90-95
                    85-90
                    80-85
                    75-80
                    70-75
                    65-70
                    55-60
                    50-55
                    45-50
                    40-45
                    35-40
                    30-35
                    25-30
                    20-25
                    15-20
                    10-15
                    5-10
                    0-5
 20 19 18 17 16 15 14 13 12 11 10 9 8 7 6 5 4 3 2 1   1 2 3 4 5 6 7 8 9 10 11 12 13 14 15
              MALE                              FEMALE
```

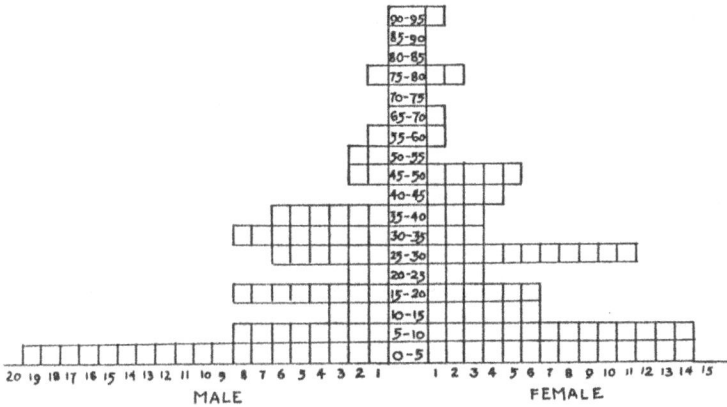

Figure 1. Population Pyramid, 1965 (Total Population: 140)

hunting territories. However, while Speck thinks that the hunting of more stationary game in the woods accounted for a Pre-Columbian family hunting territory system among the northern Algonkian, Leacock argues that the Woodland Indians practised communal nomadism and had no family hunting territory system before the onset of the fur trade. She argues convincingly that with the availability of a stable food supply provided by the local store, it became possible for individual families to occupy a certain territory without risking starvation, even if traditional subsistence game failed to appear on their territory. Furthermore, with the production of fur for trade, "the individual's most important ties, economically speaking, were transferred from *within* the band to without, and his objective relation to other band members changed from the cooperative to the competitive" (Leacock, 1954:7). Later, Knight added that "the replacement of caribou by moose and of muskets by rifles seems to have made larger hunting units and extensive separate hunts non-advantageous. It seems to have improved the opportunities for and returns from trapping – quite apart from any hypothetical acculturative shift to 'individualized,' barter economy" (1965:30).

In former times, the Naskapi hunted caribou without rifles and were dependent upon the cooperation of many people to ambush the animals, a hunting technique making any development of family hunting territories difficult. However, even after the Naskapi acquired high-powered repeating rifles, and to a significant extent abandoned the ambush technique, they still did not form a territory system. The reasons for this are found both in certain restrictions imposed by the habits of the caribou, and in the social system of the Naskapi.

Thus, because of the constant movements of the caribou over large areas and the near impossibility of predicting the time and place of their occurrence, any claim made by a small number of people to a certain territory would be rather meaningless. To be certain of caribou entering their territory in sufficient numbers and frequently enough during the year, the area would have to be so large that a small group of people would be unable to defend it from outsiders, unless it were effectively guarded by taboos. If the territory were not protected by taboos, but small enough to be protected by physical force, it would probably be too small to support any people. Hence, a group holding such a territory would be forced to seek food and/or help in neighbouring territories. In the end, this would probably develop into a sharing economy within a larger social unit, together with a break-down of any attempt to establish territorial limits.

In addition to the restrictions imposed by the habits of the caribou, the Naskapi social organization pressures them into sharing common hunting grounds. This aspect will be dealt with extensively in later chapters; suffice it to say here that those Naskapi who wish to have any prestige or influence must share with all others the spoils of their hunt. Hence, the more one has to share, the more followers and prestige one acquires; good hunters will seek many followers, while potential followers will join good hunters. As a result, Naskapi society becomes very amorphous in the sense that individual households constantly join groups with shifting memberships. In such a system, any man who tried to establish territorial limits for himself, would soon find himself alone, deserted even by his nearest relatives.

According to my informants, the traditional "home" of the Naskapi was the area around Indian House Lake (see Map 1). As Leacock (1954:5) points out, the Naskapi probably did have limits to their band territory. However, with their "home" at Indian House Lake, these limits were probably determined by what was to them familiar territory which they exploited during a yearly cycle and which normally yielded everything they needed to subsist. If necessary, they would go beyond these limits just as, according to my informants, other people from different parts of the Labrador Peninsula came to their area (cf. Strong, 1929:285).[1]

Thus, up to the beginning of the 20th century, the hunting grounds of the Naskapi centered around Indian House Lake on George River *(Moshwaw Shibo* or Barren Ground River) where the Naskapi congregated every fall to await the thousands of caribou that crossed the northern end of the lake on their yearly migration route. In their canoes, they would surround the

---

1. The absence of any exclusive territory rights is just as conspicuous today, as hunters from other communities on the Labrador coast pass through Davis Inlet to hunt in the same area as the Naskapi. Similarly, no people in the other communities on the Labrador coast claim exclusive rights to any territory for the purpose of hunting caribou. Thus, hunters all the way from Makkovik, Hopedale, and Davis Inlet will go to Nain and hunt caribou in those surroundings. As is the case with the Naskapi, the hunters of Nain have no hard feelings because of these visits.

swimming caribou and slaughter a great part of the herd. Indian groups from various parts of the Labrador-Quebec peninsula met to participate in this event, some coming all the way from Seven Islands on the Gulf of St. Lawrence. The most regular contact, however, was with the Naskapi from the Fort Chimo area, called *Waska neken Inno* by the Davis Inlet people. These two peoples often met at Indian House Lake where they intermarried.

Little is known about the social organization of the Naskapi at the time of contact. The extent to which social life in the Barren Grounds today is similar to that of former times is largely a matter of speculation. Certain changes in the technology of hunting have probably had an effect on the social organization of the hunt. For example, it is reasonable to assume that when the Naskapi hunted with spears and bows and arrows, they had a more formal and stronger system of leadership than they have today. Whether they speared the caribou from canoes in water, or shot them with bows and arrows from behind a corral-like structure,[2] the cooperation of many people was needed to drive the caribou in the right direction. This kind of hunting might have been impossible with the present day system of prestige and leadership where every man is unwilling to yield his autonomy. Considering the changes in social organization that may have taken place with the introduction of rifles and husky dogs (see ch. 2), trapping furs for individual profit, and the gradual decline of the power of the shaman, it may well be that a man who combined the skills of a good hunter and a powerful shaman was a stronger leader than the present-day leaders. However, in my opinion, the difference would be only a matter of degree, and the same basic system of prestige and leadership as it is found today also existed at the time of contact. It is doubtful if the Naskapi ever had any form of hereditary leadership. This fact may also be argued in adaptational terms: the harsh environment of the Naskapi militates against any form of permanent and hereditary leadership, while the present system may be seen as highly adaptive.

In 1833, Erlandson, a Hudson's Bay clerk in South River Post (Fort McKenzie), wrote: "These, mostly young men, are retainers of or rather drudges to the would-be great men; their employment is to attend nets and hooks and draw sledges. If any of them are industrious enough to set a trap and catch a marten, it is claimed by his master. In this state of bondage he remains till he can persuade a girl to bless him with her company; he is then a man" (Davies, 1963:222–3). This statement indicates that at least some older men had great power over young men, but it does not tell us very much about the pattern of leadership. However, it coincides with my own

---

2. My informants said that to get close enough to kill the caribou with arrows, they built a kind of corral around which the hunters would hide. The caribou were driven through a V-shaped structure of fences that led into the corral.

observations (see ch. 3 and 4) in that a man must have a wife to obtain the autonomy necessary to participate in the competition for leadership. Since Erlandson makes it explicit that it is the unmarried men who are in "this state of bondage," it might indicate that the Naskapi had, to some degree at least, the same system of leadership as they have today.

What Erlandson observed may also have been (1) young men's relationships to shamans; for example the last shaman in Davis Inlet was able to order young men to steal altar wine from the basement of the mission house and bring it to him; or (2) some form of bride service (Rogers, 1969:40).

The system of leadership as we find it today is closely tied up with the economic and ritual life of the Naskapi. This inter-relationship is expressed in a ritual called *mokoshan* (see ch. 2). There are a number of references in the literature to the animal feasts of the Indians of the Labrador Peninsula (see for example, Speck, 1935). The earliest account of a Naskapi feast involving caribou marrow, to my knowledge, is by James Clouston (Davies, 1963:36–37, 49) who explored the interior of Labrador for the Hudson's Bay Company in the years 1819–1820. His description leaves no doubt that it was the same as the *mokoshan* of contemporary Naskapi.

> "These Indians had killed two deer and as strangers had met them a feast must ensue. A long tent was erected with five fireplaces in it, and the Indians seated on each side. The venison was divided and afterwards a lump of fat, about three feet long and one foot broad and as much in depth, was shared out. This lump of fat, I was told, was the marrow fat of about two hundred deer which they had killed at one time during the winter" (p. 49).

Mokoshan is also described by Turner (1894:322–23). However, it is doubtful whether Clouston and Turner understood the significance of the ritual. Turner called it "a feast of furs" (p. 322) and said that "this feast was given by one who had been unusually successful in the capture of furbearing animals, and, to prove his wealth, displayed it before the assemblage and gave a feast in consideration of his ability" (p. 323). If this interpretation is correct, it indicates that the Naskapi, at a point after they began trapping furs, must have added the display-of-wealth aspect to the feast of *mokoshan*. For there is no doubt that the ritual which Turner observed was the same as the one described by Clouston and myself, where the essence of the ritual is a confirmation of the relationship between the hunters and the caribou spirit. "I soon departed, and attempted to take the remnant of the pemmican with me. This was instantly forbidden, and information given me that by so doing I should cause all the deer to desert the vicinity, and thus make the people starve."[3]

---

3. Cf. also Strong, 1929:285.

Turner's observation is interesting because in the present-day *mokoshan* only the caribou, and no other animals, are involved in the ritual. Furthermore, the display of inequality as Turner describes it would be impossible in today's *mokoshan*. His interpretation of *mokoshan* indicates that the leadership role was stronger and recognized more than it is today (cf. ch. 2 and 3).

The Naskapi, or *Moshwaw Inno,* were and are perhaps the least known of the Indians on the Labrador Peninsula. Although the French and the English traded on the southern shores of the Peninsula as early as the sixteenth century gradually moving northwards into Hudson Bay and along the Labrador coast, the interior of the northern part of the Labrador Peninsula and its people remained unknown for a long time.

The missionaries who came to Labrador also started their work in the south. As early as 1633, the Jesuit priest Le Jeune wintered with a band of Montagnais Indians in southwestern Labrador (see Thwaites, 1906). However, it took a long time before the missionaries reached the northern Naskapi; although the Moravians established themselves in Nain in Northern Labrador in 1771 (Hiller, 1971), they worked only among the Eskimos, while the Indians in the interior were left relatively alone. One of my Naskapi informants, who was fifty-seven years old, told me that he travelled with his father from Fort Chimo to Seven Islands to "see the priest."

The Hudson's Bay Company, however, wished to extend its business northwards and into the interior where some thought that the Indians were living "in great plenty, not one in twenty of whom ever troubled to visit a European trading post" (Williams, 1963:XXXV). It was believed that by their usual method, they would be able to reach and exploit these Indians. Thus, Captain Coats writes in the middle of the eighteenth century, "those few that has frequented the settlements, begin to like our commodities better; their women like our nicknacks and guegaws, and the men begin to love brandy, bread, and tobacco, so that a little address and management will bring these happy drones out of their profound lethargy" (*op. cit.*:XXXV).

Nearly three quarters of a century later, the northern Indians were still left alone. They had by this time obtained white man's goods, either by direct trading or through Indian middlemen, but the Hudson's Bay Company had not yet managed "to tie them to the posts." In 1814, an employee of the company wrote about the Indians near Great Whale River: "Nothing but necessity or extreme want, will ever produce a spirit of exertion, in such Indians as these; their dependence on us is very trifling, the Deer (caribou) furnishes them with both food and raiment, and so long as they can procure a supply of Powder, Shot, Tobacco and a hearty swill of grog at times, their wants are wholly supplied" (*op. cit.*:XXXVII).

In 1819, the Hudson's Bay Company seriously began to explore the northern interior for the purpose of setting up trading posts. They were stimulated in this effort by their desire to intercept the Indian trade with the North West Company and the Eskimo trade with the Moravians. In 1830, they established Fort Chimo (*op. cit.*) and in 1831, a trading post in Davis Inlet. A few years later, they also established several posts in the interior but they were short-lived as they turned out to be highly unprofitable.

The managers of these posts had difficulty in making the Naskapi trap as much fur as they wanted them to. The manager at the newly established Fort Chimo complained that "their only talk is about Deer and deer hunting" (*op. cit.*:LXVIII). The problem of turning the Naskapi into good fur trappers is understandable considering their crucial dependence upon caribou combined with the inability of the Europeans to move food supplies into the country to feed the Indians, should they engage extensively in trapping. Neglecting an opportunity to hunt caribou for the sake of obtaining fur-bearing animals could be fatal for them. This, however, was of little concern to the traders. Williams writes: "Like most other Company traders who came into contact with the interior Indians, Finlayson (the first manager of the Fort Chimo Post, author's note) showed little real understanding of the relationship between the yearly routine of the Naskapi and the implacable environment in which they struggled to keep alive. His normal reaction was irritation at their unwillingness to make an abrupt change in their way of life to suit European trade requirements. However, he was unable to deal with them as sharply as he wished, because he was dependent on them for fresh meat ..." (Williams, 1963:LXVI).

The traders were well aware of how they disrupted the Naskapi yearly round of activities. In 1833, Erlandson wrote from South River Post (Fort McKenzie):

"The returns amount to 250 skins MBr. and 130 deerskins. This is a mere trifle considering the expenses incurred, and I regret that I cannot hold out prospects of better success next year, supposing the post would be kept up and that the same Indians would again trade here. It was by great persuasion and extraordinary encouragement I induced them to look after martens in the early part of winter. Subsequently some of them were starving, which they blamed me for, saying that I enticed them to hunt furs when they could have killed abundance of deer; they then came to me not only expecting, but demanding, food which I was unable to supply them with. Now, said they, we hunted skins for you, we are hungry and you have nothing to give us, do you expect that we will again hunt for you? There are beaver up this river and a few also up the Natchecagamy River, but they will not kill them unless I reckon each large skin as two skins; but the truth is they are too indolent. From these combined circumstances it will not I think be difficult to anticipate the amount of the returns of an ensuing year" (Davies, 1963:221–22).

12

It may be inferred from this quotation that the Naskapi retained much of their independence of the white man since they lived in such a marginal environment with regard to fur-bearing animals. In comparison to most other Indian groups further south, this is true to some extent. The Naskapi continued their nomadic existence as caribou hunters in the interior of northern Labrador until approximately 1916, when the great caribou herds passing through Indian House Lake changed their migration route (Strong, 1929). This caused hunger and near starvation for the expectant Indians. The Indians then moved to the coast to seek help from the stores operated by the Hudson's Bay Company. The *Waskaneken Inno* moved to Fort Chimo while most of the *Moshwaw Inno* moved to Voisey's Bay and some to Davis Inlet. Since then the Naskapi have seldom ventured into George River, but formed closer ties to the stores and the mission stations.

In 1924, a Roman Catholic missionary came to Davis Inlet on a summer visit where he appointed an English-speaking Naskapi as chief and promised to come back every summer if the chief could gather all the Naskapi from Voisey's Bay and Davis Inlet for the event. From 1927 on, the missionary made annual summer visits and gradually all the Naskapi became tied to Davis Inlet. There has been a missionary all year round in Davis Inlet since 1952.

The Naskapi at Fort Chimo have been moved to the mining area at Knob Lake. Although some of the Davis Inlet Naskapi have relatives among them, they never meet. Today, the Davis Inlet people have contact with the Indians at North West River, with whom they also intermarry.

As we have seen, traditionally, the Naskapi hunted in the interior. Although they had regularly travelled to the coast to trade their furs with the Hudson's Bay Company since the middle of the last century, they apparently never undertook seasonal migrations to exploit the renewable resources of the sea (cf. Strong, 1929; Kleivan, 1966). Even after their forced move to the coast in 1916, they kept their orientation towards the interior. Caribou and other land animals were still of great importance to the Naskapi, not only as food but also as part of their social and ritual life.

However, having moved their families to the coast, it was then a large undertaking to go inland. At that time, the Naskapi had few dogs and this meant that it took a long time to travel into the Barrens. Very little store-bought food could be carried on the sleds to guard against hunger. These factors, coupled with the greater uncertainty of finding caribou after the herds had changed their migration routes, meant that the Naskapi stayed closer to the coast and relied on the store and its supplies whenever necessary.

The Hudson's Bay Company wanted furs in exchange for their goods, but it "had an agreement with the Newfoundland authorities which, in brief, worked like this: the Company had the right to import all wares duty-free to the stations in Labrador. In return, it was to assume the responsibility for those who needed help, i.e. give a kind of public relief" (Kleivan, 1966).[4] In 1934, the issuing of relief was taken over by the Newfoundland rural police (the province's equivalent to the RCMP). Finally, in 1942, the Hudson's Bay Company gave up its business in Northern Labrador and the Newfoundland government took over the trade and the responsibility for the welfare of the population.[5] Then in 1949, Newfoundland became the tenth province of Canada and the population began receiving federal family allowances and old age pensions.[6] In 1957, the Newfoundland government extended unemployment insurance to cod and char fishermen of Northern Labrador, but excluded the Naskapi from this category. Apparently, the government did not regard them as fishermen at this time and granted them welfare payments, instead.[7]

In July, 1951, the United States started to construct a radar base at Hopedale, only one day's travel by dog sled from Davis Inlet. This meant money through wage labour; people were attracted to this opportunity all the way from Nain, Nutak, and Hebron. The Naskapi, however, never took advantage of it although they knew about it.

When living on the coast, the Naskapi kept to the bays, utilizing the resources of the land and supplementing their meagre incomes with government relief. They partook neither in the char nor cod fisheries, and they rarely used the seal for their own consumption. They had, by now, developed a great taste for alcohol. At the time of the arrival of the present missionary in Davis Inlet in 1955, the Naskapi were spending the summer season in Sango Bay, mainly living off relief and drinking. The Naskapi themselves relate that all the men and most of the women used to get drunk almost every day. Even the children from ten years and up were drinking alcohol.[8] The missionary, whose goal was to make the Naskapi into "good Christians," saw that his first task was to bring this drinking to an end.

---

4. According to Jenness (1965:60), the Hudson's Bay Company *had* to pay regular import duties, and the relief they distributed consisted mainly of a monthly ration of biscuits and tea which the Newfoundland government paid for.
5. For a fuller treatment of the administration on the coast, see Jenness, 1965.
6. "In 1951 Newfoundland openly acknowledged the deterioration of Northern Labrador's economy by transferring its administration from the Department of Natural Resources to the Department of Public Welfare, which created for the task a special organization entitled 'Division of Northern Labrador Affairs'" (Jenness, 1965). D.N.L.A. has recently changed its name to Northern Labrador Service Division.
7. In 1948, the government had moved all the Naskapi north to the Eskimo village of Nutak where they were supposed to fish. However, both the Eskimos and the Indians disliked this arrangement and the latter also took a dislike to the barren coastal environment. After a while, the Naskapi simply disappeared. The government was left puzzled until the Indians reappeared at Davis Inlet five months later.
8. The alcohol was, and still is in the form of spruce beer which they brew out of the juice of boiled spruce branches, sugar, and yeast. As far as I know, the Naskapi did not make any alcoholic drinks before contact with Europeans.

It is largely due to the missionary that the Naskapi gradually have come to participate more actively in a money economy. By rendering a variety of services, he has bound the Naskapi closer to the mission so that today, they spend most of the summer in Davis Inlet. By acquiring a sound knowledge of the Naskapi language, it has been possible for the missionary to play the role of middleman and broker between the Naskapi and the storekeeper, government officials, and other representatives of the Canadian society (the role of the missionary will be treated further in Chapter 6). For the isolated Naskapi with their poor knowledge of English, the missionary facilitates a broader contact with the outside world and new possibilities for acquiring its goods and services. With their growing desire for material goods, grew also their need for cash.

In 1961, the missionary and the government decided to encourage the Naskapi to fish cod. The government gave the Naskapi small punts which they could use to jig in the bays. Furthermore, relief was cut off during the cod season to encourage fishing. In the second year of the scheme, the missionary gave an outboard engine to a Naskapi who was to repay him when he had saved enough money. The proud new owner took off from shore where the whole village was assembled, waving and cheering for the first "motorized" Naskapi. Today (1968), almost every household has an outboard engine, and eight men have bought bigger motorboats. Except for one motorboat which was acquired with help from the storekeeper, all of them were bought by the missionary who gave them to the Naskapi on the condition that they save money and repay him. With motorboats at their disposal, the Naskapi could handle cod traps, of which the government (in 1968) provided two.

Through the missionary, the Naskapi also expressed a desire to live in houses. The government was in favour of this and in the period between 1966 and 1969, a new community was built; the first Naskapi moved into houses in the fall of 1967. This present settlement of Davis Inlet is located on the eastern shore of Iluikoyak Island, one of the inner forested islands on the coast of Labrador (see Map 2). The houses are located at the foot of a hill which rises steeply to the west, and they are protected from the worst winds by the spruce trees which grow around them. About one hundred yards below the village to the east, stretches a sandy beach that curves, forming a quiet cove. In the summer, the Naskapi put out their nets from this cove and catch a fair amount of arctic char. From the beach, one looks across a mile of wafer to Ukasiksalik Island and in the spring, one can see seals basking in the sun; when the ice starts to break up, schools of seals can sometimes be seen in the narrow rattle between Ukasiksalik and Iluikoyak Islands, looking southeast from the village. Travelling through that rattle and two miles further south, one comes to the former site of Davis Inlet which was abandoned during the summer of 1967.[9] Here, except for one family, all the Naskapi lived in tents (see Chapter 6).

The community of Davis Inlet is relatively isolated, the nearest neighbours being the Eskimos and settlers in Nain and Hopedale, sixty miles north and south of Davis Inlet, respectively. Contact with these communities is limited to a few Naskapi who take a trip by dog sled during the winter to buy huskies or to experience the excitement of going to another community. The nearest Indian community is North West River which is about 150 miles south of Davis Inlet; occasionally, a Naskapi will go to the nearest hospital which is located in that community, but only seldom does one take the costly trip by boat or plane merely to visit relatives there. Except for Goose Bay and Happy Valley which lie close to North West River, no other communities than those mentioned above are visited by the Naskapi on their own initiative.

Commercial transportation facilities along the coast of Labrador consist of two coastal steamers that run between the provincial capital of St. John's and Nain, visiting the communities every tenth day in the ice-free season from the end of June to the end of October. In the period between the freeze-up of coastal waters and the break-up of the ice in the spring, a scheduled mail plane stationed at Goose Bay serves the communities in northern Labrador once a week, weather permitting. The types of aircraft employed are the small Beaver and Otter planes. They take passengers only if there is room after the mail has been loaded.

---

9. The move from the old village to the new took place while the author was in the field.

Part II: The World of the Hunter

Nomads in the Barren Lands

2

In the spring, when the Naskapi travel towards the coast and Davis Inlet, they look forward to meeting people they have not seen for a long time, and to visiting the store where they can buy all the goods which they have to ration or do completely without in the Barren Grounds. Indeed, if the date of departure depended on snow and ice conditions, most of the Naskapi could stay a month longer in the Barrens than they do and still travel down to the coast by dog sled. However, in their deliberations, they all give as reasons for leaving that it will be good to see people again, and to have plenty of tobacco, tea, and beer.

Yet, after only a few weeks in Davis Inlet, both men and women start talking about the Barren Grounds as being a much better place to live than Davis Inlet. "The salt water," they claim, "is no good." Very soon the men start leaving on short caribou hunting trips in groups of two or three, abandoning cod fishing and other money-earning activities.

During August, the hunting trips become more frequent until the Naskapi finally take their families into the interior sometime in September or October. The sea is not yet frozen, and so the Naskapi usually load their families, dogs and sleds, and other equipment onto their big trap boats and small punts and travel into the bays. When the first ice begins to form, they pull up onto the beaches and establish their autumn camps. The swift-flowing rivers are not yet frozen and the men pursue their hunting activities close to the salt water; they hunt black bear, porcupine, and ptarmigan, and some trap for mink and fox. The most important food resources, however, are seal and arctic char which they catch in nets under the ice of the lake. The seal meat and fat are fed to the dogs that have been on a starvation diet throughout the summer. They are now well-fed and quickly regain the strength necessary for the tasks that lie ahead of them.

Finally, the rivers are frozen and the Naskapi make their way into the Barrens. At Christmas, most of the families return to Davis Inlet to celebrate, meet people they have not seen for several months, and buy a fresh supply of goods at the store. Weather permitting, they leave for the Barrens again before the New Year. If the caribou are plentiful, only the oldest people stay behind in Davis Inlet; if they are scarce, a few young people may also choose to spend the winter on the coast.

At different intervals, small groups of families leave Davis Inlet with their heavily loaded dog sleds. They start off on the windswept surface of the sea ice forming a string of dogs, sleds, and running people. They follow in the tracks of those who left earlier in the morning or a day or two before them. About noon, they reach the head of Sango Bay where a settler family lives. Here they all stop and are treated to bread and tea. Since the old settler no longer uses his dogs in the middle of the winter (his son owns a motor toboggan), he lends his whole dog team to the Naskapi, who in return feed the dogs. On their way back from the Barren Grounds, the Naskapi again stop in Sango for tea and bread. In this way, the Naskapi-speaking settler family gets news about the conditions in the interior as well as some choice pieces of meat. The Naskapi enjoyed this relationship, but the second winter of my fieldwork, the settler family moved to the community of Hopedale and their house in Sango stood empty and cold. The Naskapi all regretted this: "No more of Charlotte's tea and bread."

Not too far past the settler's house, the journey up the river begins. Here the snow lies deep, and the pace of dogs and men becomes slower but steady. The younger children become weary and find a place on top of the sled. Their fathers start pulling to help the dogs along.

Only two generations[1] ago, most Naskapi pulled their belongings on light toboggans without any help from dogs. Today, every household has a team of huskies pulling a heavy sled, both items adopted from the Eskimos on the coast of Labrador. The sled[2] is between twelve and fifteen feet long, with two heavy iron-shod runners to which cross-bars are lashed the full length of the sled. The Naskapi make the sleds themselves, but have to buy the runners, iron shoes, and rope. This sled is excellent on ice and hard-packed surfaces, but is heavy and difficult to manoeuver in loose and deep snow. A team of four or five dogs can pull a maximum of six hundred pounds up the rivers into the Barrens.

The number of dogs a man owns varies from year to year and only a few Naskapi try to keep a permanent team for any number of years. One family may travel into the Barrens with only three dogs while another may have as

---

1. This I estimate on the basis of different life stories told by my informants. Strong (1929:287) mentions a similar date for the introduction of dog sleds.
2. The Naskapi word for this type of sled is *atabaskoots,* but they also use the Eskimo word *kamotik.*

many as ten. On the average, the hunters have about five dogs each. Although a few are proud of their dogs and feed them well all year round, most Naskapi treat them roughly; the main reason for this is that they regard the dogs as a nuisance in the summer, because they have to be fed even though they do not work. Their general attitude towards dogs approaches that which they have towards their material equipment which I shall discuss later in this chapter. The result is that one may see a family sled being pulled by the husband together with two or three weak dogs, while his wife pushes from behind – all the way from Davis Inlet and 150 miles inland.

The sled is loaded with their needs for the winter: two axes (one for the husband and one for the wife), a saw, rope, cooking utensils, sewing needles, and other small tools; the bottom of an oil drum serves as a pot for cooking dog food: seal meat and fat boiled with cornmeal. They also carry a considerable amount of staples bought at the store. An average family may have 100 to 150 pounds of flour. A man who drinks a lot of spruce beer may take as much as 75 pounds of sugar. Lard, margarine, and salt pork also add significantly to the weight, as does a gramophone or radio and all the other small luxury items that contribute to the enjoyment of a household. All these supplies are carefully piled onto the sled and lashed tightly with a rope. The tent is then secured over everything.

The tent is sewn together by a woman in a few hours; it is made out of the cheapest cotton duck obtained at the store. In summer, the rain drizzles through and in winter, it gives only moderate protection against the winds.

The stove is tied to the top of the load at the back of the sled. The husband makes it out of a thin iron sheet which he buys at the store. This stove has a perfect draught and can give off tremendous heat, keeping the tent fairly warm even when the temperature creeps down to fifty below. Also fastened to the load outside the tent canvas are the firearms, one of the axes, a tea kettle, mugs, and the family's snowshoes which they put on and take off depending on the snow cover. Finally, on top of the whole load the children sit. The babies are covered in blankets and secured to the load completely underneath the tent canvas. They are given a little bag of caribou skin, called *piwas,* filled with milk which they suck.

When the snow is loose and deep, the narrow runners of the heavily laden sleds sink and make it hard for men and dogs to move. Then the women and older children have to walk on their snowshoes in front of the sleds to make a trail. The men work beside the sleds, pulling and pushing to keep them on the trail. Every now and then, the sleds get stuck and the dogs stop. The men must push and pull to get it going again, continually shouting at the dogs lo keep them working.

During the late autumn, the water level in the rivers may fall drastically, causing the formation of several levels of ice. Occasionally a sled breaks through the top layer and falls five or six feet down to the next layer of ice. Then trees have to be cut so that the sled can be hoisted out of the hole.

Along most of the routes used, some hillsides are so steep that the Naskapi must unload half their supplies and make two trips. After making camp close to such a hill, the men must go off with their dogs and take half the load to the other side of the hill, often returning in the dark.

Going down steep hills in the woods is a risky undertaking. The trails are narrow and crooked and the heavy sleds pick up considerable speed, even though the Naskapi throw loops of dog chains around the front ends of the runners in order to reduce it. The driver steers the sled by pushing and pulling the front in the direction to and from him; to make the turns, he lies on the sled and kicks off from the trees. At the same time, he must shout at the dogs to make them run as fast as they can, or else the sled would overtake them. Sometimes a hill or a rapid in the river is so steep that he must let the dogs loose. With the driver clinging to the sled trying to keep it on its course, the sled catapults down the hill in a cloud of snow.

The Naskapi seldom help each other when they are travelling. Each family is on its own, and nobody worries if one family does not reach camp in the evening. Whatever the reason for not catching up, they are expected to be able to handle the situation alone, and nobody will wait for them the next day. Only once have I seen the Naskapi worry about people on the trail. From a camp in the Barrens, a father and son left for the one-hundred mile trip to the store at Davis Inlet. After one week, the average time men take to cover this distance, they had not returned, and after three weeks, the people in the camp began to worry. Tension rose with every passing day. The wife of the man was overcome with hysterical fits and a few days later, the daughter fell into similar fits. The day that a sled was spotted on the lake, the whole camp ran to it and binoculars were passed from hand to hand. Great was the relief when it turned out to be the missing father and son. What happened was that they had become sick with the flu and had to rest every second day of the journey.

Also, only once have I experienced people asking for help. It happened when an elderly couple ran into difficulty while making their way through deep loose snow in the woods on their way to our camp. When the man arrived at the camp after dark, alone and on foot, he asked his son to help him bring his sled and wife back. Not only the son but all the men helped while the old man remained in camp.

The Naskapi always keep a keen trained eye on their surroundings while travelling. Continuously, they scan the trees and the bushes along the rivers and hills of the near and distant landscape for signs of life; they can spot in a flash the tracks of ptarmigan on a river bank or the antlers of a caribou above a hilltop. They travel in single file, and every now and then, a man will indicate to the others that he has seen something. If someone can take over handling the sled, a hunter may make a quick detour to shoot some ptarmigan, or track down a porcupine from the teeth marks left on a tree. The ptarmigan are plucked on the move and may be eaten for lunch. No matter how early in the morning the Naskapi start out, they never take a break before noon. Then they stop for fifteen to twenty minutes and in an instant have a roaring fire with tea kettles over it.

Reckoning that other people may follow parts of the same route as themselves, the Naskapi leave messages behind for them. They may leave a piece of paper inside a parcel and attach it to a bush, or make a cut in a tree and leave a note there saying where they are going, who they think are in front of them on the trail, the condition of the ice and snow, and so on. (They write in Naskapi using the English alphabet.) Whenever they pass an abandoned camp, they stop to examine it to find out whose it was and how long ago it was inhabited. In this manner, the Naskapi manage to keep track of each other to a certain degree.

The Naskapi never take unnecessary risks while travelling. With their families present, they must choose routes where they can reach a stand of forest if a storm should erupt. This precaution is not as important when only men are travelling, as they put up with a lot of bad weather in order to gain speed and time. Only twice have I seen men turn back because of a storm and drifting snow. Both times, the visibility was so poor that we could not see the first dog in the team and the wind so strong that it was difficult to walk. Knowing the features of the landscape, and making use of many signs, the Naskapi can find their way through almost any kind of weather. They pride themselves in having this ability, and many stories focus on this topic.

To illustrate the endurance and stamina which the Naskapi possess and the speed with which they travel, I present the following account of a trip I shared with them. From a camp one hundred miles in the interior, the men were about to leave their families and travel down to Davis Inlet to buy "store food." Before our departure, the men talked about earlier trips from the same area, especially of one which was made in five days (return) when Frank had been the *wotshimao*[3] (literally first man) or leader, and therefore received the credit for the speedy trip. But this time, a young man said he wanted to lead the way, declaring that he would travel very rapidly. For several days he went around and spoke about the speed with which he would make the journey.

One day without warning, four men left the camp. The next day, the young man, his brother, and I got up at one o'clock in the morning and set

---

3. The pattern of leadership will be dealt with further in ch. 3.

off in the moonlight in one sled. The young man was the leader. Frank and his brother started a little later in another sled and caught up with us at 8 a.m. With every man taking turns running and sitting on the sled, we travelled non-stop until noon. After the usual fifteen minute tea break, we continued on until five o'clock, by which time we were in the woods where the snow was loose and deep making movement difficult. Hoping to get on to a harder surface, we kept running in snow as high as the middle of our thighs without stopping to put on our snowshoes. Finally, the young *wotshimao* stopped and hinted that either we should camp then or try to reach Sango Bay that night. He asked Frank and his brother who were older and experienced men what they thought we should do. They answered that it was he who was *wotshimao,* and that it was his decision. Although it was getting dark and everybody was tired, the young leader said that *he* could travel on, but that the dogs were tired. Everybody agreed that it might be too hard for the dogs to continue and that perhaps we should make a camp. Although it was his privilege to decide upon a camp site, the young man felt insecure and left it up to Frank and his brother to find a suitable place to put up the tent.

We moved on until we came to a creek where we could find water and a dry place for the tent. Even in snow cover, the Naskapi are able to judge if the ground underneath is wet, icy, or dry. If a tent is erected on the wrong spot it becomes damp and cold. Preferably, the Naskapi erect their tents parallel to a river or along the beach of a lake.

It was dark by the time we found a place to camp. One man started to prepare the tent floor by shovelling away some of the loose snow with his snowshoe, and then tramping it down to a firmer surface. Another started to cut firewood; a goodly sized tree – cut and split into small logs – is needed for the evening and morning fires. The rest of us went to fetch small spruce trees to make the twenty or so poles necessary to hold up the walls and roof of the dome-shaped tent. The frame is made in the following way: the trees are dragged over to the tent floor where the twigs are lopped off, thus making a first layer of insulating branches. All the poles are then pushed together to form a circle. Three poles are erected: one on each side of the door and one at the back of the tent. Across from them are laid the poles that are the foundation of the flat roof. Later, the stovepipe will come up between them. Finally, the tent is thrown over this framework.

As soon as we had the stove in position, we got a roaring fire going that spat a rain of sparks into the dark night. Meat and tea kettles were put on and soon the tent was filled with the smell of boiling meat. But before we could eat, we had to bring all the baggage into the tent to prevent the dogs from tearing it up, tie the dogs up, and cook their food. During the day's travel, we had shot a few ptarmigan which we now plucked, mixing the feathers with the dog food – a method which slows down the digestive process. To this end the Naskapi also use caribou hair and lichen. When the food had cooled off, the men unhitched the hungry howling dogs. One man stood over each tray of food with stick in hand to keep them away until they were all loose. Then they were allowed to plunge into the "porridge," each one fighting to get the most. (It is necessary to beat the strongest so that the weaker ones can get their share.) Afterwards, the dogs were caught and chained for the night.

Our work for the day was not yet finished. To make the next day's travel easier, we put on our snowshoes and tramped down a trail several miles through the woods until we came to the harder surface of the big river that runs into Sango Bay. We were back in camp by one o'clock at night and went to sleep. We had then been working for twenty-four hours.

At three o'clock, after two hours sleep, we got up and started a fire in the stove. At six, the sleds were packed and we were on the trail again. Soon we passed an abandoned camp site where a piece of paper was spotted, tied to a pole. It stated that the author of the note had taken some of the caribou meat belonging to a man named Fred. The reaction among the men was that "it was not good to take other people's meat." Not long after, we passed a tree with a big chip cut off its trunk. There Fred had written that he was travelling in such deep snow that he had to leave three caribou behind. (Later he went to fetch the carcasses from Davis Inlet.)

That day, we reached Davis Inlet at 1:30 p.m. and went directly to the store to buy our goods. Staying overnight, we got up at 3 a.m. and left the community at 6 a.m. All nine men from our camp were now together (later, we were joined by four men from a nearby camp). The *wotshimao* for our group was now Noel, the leader of the group who had left the Barrens before us. Everybody said that he would travel very quickly. With heavily loaded sleds we kept moving until seven o'clock, when Noel decided to make camp. Three men were now limping beside the sleds (including the anthropologist). One man had great pains from a lump as big as a fist behind his knee. They all praised Noel for his fast travelling and as he was not a tall man, they repeated again and again, laughing, that he was "a short big wotshimao" (*apesasho meshao wotshimao*).

After setting up camp and feeding the dogs, all nine of us settled down for the night in one small tent. When men are travelling without their families, they prefer to stay in one tent. They boil a lot of meat and fry big pieces of ribs on sticks beside the stove. They eat, talk, and laugh for hours, relating anything from hunting stories to lewd jokes (which they would not tell in front of their women). They thoroughly enjoy their men's culture as long as they are alone. Finally, we went to sleep, lying curled up side by side.

At five in the morning we left camp. Not long after, one man went through the ice and got wet up to his waist. Everybody laughed, but we all travelled on until we reached the families that same day, after dark and in a snow storm. By the end the dogs were so tired that we had to push the sleds over every other snow drift. It had taken us four days to travel two hundred miles.

In the spring, when the Naskapi travel back to Davis Inlet, the trip is not easier. From their camp in the Barrens, the men leave first with a load of meat, taking it as far as possible and returning to camp at night. The next day, they travel with their families and camp possessions as far as the women and children allow. After setting up camp, the men return for the meat and then take it past the camp as far as possible, returning to their families late at night. In this shuttling manner, they travel all the way to Davis Inlet. Even then, the amount of meat they manage to take is limited to three or four caribou per sled.

In this nomadic way of life, the women are no less tough and persevering than the men. After a long hard day of travelling, they always have the strength necessary to build the camp together with their husbands and to take care of the children. Every now and then they travel in a pregnant condition and give birth to a child in the Barren Grounds. Although the birth itself is dramatized by all the women in the camp, it does not hinder the movement of the people to any extent. Once we travelled with a pregnant woman who was about to deliver any day and we had to set up camp in a blizzard that blew up suddenly. She went into labour the same night in a wind-blown chilly tent which she and her family shared with her brother. No men except her brother were allowed in the tent, while her husband and older children had to stay with another family. All the women in camp stayed with her a day and night until the child was born the second day. The women said she had been very sick – so sick that she had almost died. (This is a common claim when a person is not in a normal physical state.) Two days after the birth, all the families left the camp except the family with the new-born child who left on the third day, and caught up with us on the fourth. Even though the mother sat on the sled most of the time, she walked up the hills and even helped pull it.

When travelling with an infant, a woman uses every opportunity to nurse it. As soon as the men stop the sleds to straighten out the harness, or investigate some caribou tracks, the woman uncovers her baby's face from underneath the tent canvas to feed it. Even in the worst weather, she bends over the sled with her back against the wind and the drifting snow and nurses her baby.

Meeting people in the Barrens is a great event. The excitement is immense in the camp and among the arrivals. Usually the children who are out playing discover the approaching people. Shouting and screaming, they announce their observation. Their parents come running out, also shouting elatedly in anticipation of new faces and news from Davis Inlet or other camps in the interior. Once the identity of the visitors is guessed, their closest relatives run back to their tents to put meat in the kettle and prepare tea.

Sometimes the communal meal called *mokoshan* is held immediately upon the arrival of new people in a camp. Otherwise, the visitors duck into one of their relatives' tents to eat and talk. The cold children are affectionately attended to by the womenfolk, and then the arrivals look for a good place to erect their tent(s). They will already have been given gifts of meat by many of the people in the camp. If there is enough caribou, they receive whole carcasses, including the skins.

If one stood on a hilltop overlooking the Barrens, one would spot a small cluster of tents nestled in a stand of trees. Smoke rising through the cold air and the echo of children's voices at play indicate a community lying below. From this vantage point, one sees sled tracks here and there leading out of the forest only to be lost on the hard surface of the Barrens. These are the tracks of men who have brought home caribou they have shot. Descending into the forest, one finds the tracks of men and women who have been out to fetch firewood or fresh spruce twigs to lay on the floor. Everywhere there are snowshoe trails and stumps from trees that have been cut. Then suddenly, one stumbles upon a tent surrounded by dogs curled up in their chains. A few pups wander around, now nuzzling their mother, now sneaking into the tent only to be thrown out yelping into the snow. Occasionally, a few loose dogs start a fight over food found in the camp, causing the rest of the dogs to become restless.

Close to the entrance of the tent are the firearms of the hunter stacked in the snow against the tent wall. One will also find a pole on which the family snowshoes hang, safely out of reach of the dogs who would eat the rawhide meshwork. On a big scaffold erected near the tent, the household stores whole carcasses of caribou along with antlers and bone splinters.

Entering the tent, immediately inside the door one finds caribou hanging from poles above the stove. The meat is dried in this way, the choicest parts thus prepared being the rib pieces (ribs removed) and the tenderloin (which is usually pounded afterwards). Other delicacies from the caribou hanging further away from the stove are rectums, fetuses, and blood which is kept inside the eviscerated stomachs of the caribou. There are also caribou heads which will eventually be fried. One may find several legs thawing out and whole carcasses stacked up against the wall to keep them from freezing solidly outdoors. Lying around the perimeter of the tent are most of the possessions of the household such as blankets, clothing, and boxes containing store goods. Moccasins and mittens, sinews, and other odds and ends hang from the wall poles.

Formally, the master of the tent has his place immediately to the left of the entrance. However, this custom is not always adhered to and one usually finds the family members scattered around, occupied with their different chores. Generally, the Naskapi have a lot of leisure time since they often have enough meat in the camp to be able to refrain from hunting. The men spend most of this time visiting and talking with one another. They also make the frames and rawhide meshwork for the middle part of the snowshoes (women make the meshwork for the ends), fashion crooked knives, repair the dog harnesses, and perform similar chores.

Usually it is the men who get the firewood, either carrying it on their shoulders or having it hauled by dog sled. However, if the men are occupied with hunting for days on end, the women have to bring home the firewood. (In bad weather, or if no firewood can be found nearby, it is invariably the men's job.) The husband's main responsibility, however, is that of provider – for his own family, and sometimes for others. Alone, or together with other men, he hunts in the surrounding barren land.

The women always remain near the tents where they must keep the fire going, care for the children, and mend the family's moccasins and clothing. They always have meat and tea ready when their husbands come home tired and hungry from hunting. Much of their time is spent in the laborious task of tanning caribou hides. After the thin layer of fat is chopped off, the hide and the hairs removed, the hide is washed and frozen many times before it is finally smoked.

As we shall see later, the division of labour between men and women is an important aspect of Naskapi life. However, there are no taboos connected with this division; the women are allowed to hunt and fish, and the men may tan skins and sew moccasins.

Naskapi children are full of vitality. They spend most of the day playing outside, even in the coldest weather. Every now and then they rush into the nearest tent to warm their hands over the stove, and take a bite of meat and a sip of tea before they vanish again. They slide on small toboggans, sometimes hitching young pups to them and mimicking their fathers both in action and in swearing at the pups to get them to pull. The children also enjoy chasing squirrels and each other, sneaking around with bows and arrows and playing "cowboys and Indians" – modelled on the movies they have seen in Davis Inlet. During the evenings or in bad weather, they play inside the tents. Then their parents often join in their play. Their fathers make whatever they need, whether it is for the pin and cup game, the button game, or "whirligigs." Favourite pastimes for both children and grown-ups are making string figures and "shooting" caribou made from wooden chips.

The Naskapi treat their children permissively. Growing up in tents, the children are given much freedom to do what they like and are seldom scolded. Material goods such as gramophones and records are broken, smashed deliberately, or thrown away by the children without their parents reprimanding them. The children are taught to give away things they value to other children who want them. The Naskapi are very fond of their children and conflicts often arise between parents because of one child hitting another. Parents do not tolerate other parents' scolding their children.

While a girl starts helping her mother with small chores from the age of six or seven, a boy is not expected to do any work before he is about ten years of age. Then he begins to cut a little wood and train himself to drive a dog sled. He starts to accompany his father on short trips when he goes off to fetch caribou he has shot in the Barrens. He comes home proudly and talks about the caribou herds he has seen. The men acknowledge his deeds and say to him: "*miam napesh tchin*"; that is, "you are a fine little man".

Between every tent in the camp there are well-trodden paths in the snow from people visiting each other. There is always a social activity going on in a Naskapi camp such as a communal meal, ritual, or a game of checkers. Every now and then, the whole camp joins in a squirrel chase. It starts with children who have spotted a squirrel and are trying to catch it and before long their parents and the rest of the camp join them. The point is to get the squirrel without shooting it. Since the squirrel hides in treetops, the men fetch their axes and start chopping trees down. Before one tree has reached the ground, the squirrel is in the top of another. Thus, one after the other, huge trees crash to the ground amidst shouting and laughter from both the children and their parents.

The Naskapi make a similar exalted chase after the otter, although here it is only the men and boys who participate. Somebody discovers that an otter is living in the creek system of a swamp. The news is shouted throughout the camp, and soon all the men and boys join the hunt with shovels, axes, and sticks. All the creeks in the swamp may be dug up before they give up the first day. A few men may put out traps for the night, and the next day everybody is out digging again. However, the result is usually negative, the otter having made his escape during the night. Should anybody see the otter flee, he may run after the animal a whole day trying to hit it on the head with an axe.

The chase is important for the Naskapi. Seldom do they wait for the animal to approach them, but rather try to sneak up on it, whether it is a goose, duck, seal, or caribou. Unlike the Eskimo, the Naskapi do not have the patience to stand at the edge of the ice, waiting for a seal to pop its head up.

The Naskapi day begins with the first hint of daylight. Out of their blankets, they immediately put on their footgear (they sleep in their clothes). On awaking, a man seldom knows what he will be doing that day, as he must consider several factors: first, if the weather is fit for hunting or any

27

other outdoor activity; second, what the other hunters want to do. If some want to go hunting, others may want to join them. Then, if all the hunters want to go out together, it is a question of who will be the leader. On the other hand, if they split into several groups, each going in different directions, there will be several first men. In this case, the individual hunter has to choose which men he wants to go with, decide whether he wants to be *wotshimao,* and if so, persuade the others to let him. All these questions have to be resolved each morning.

Even if a few men, or all of them made some kind of a decision the evening before, one can never be sure that someone has not changed his mind. It is important, then, to see what sort of preparations different people are making at daybreak. Sometimes the wife or children, but more often the husband himself, will walk around the camp to gather information. The best hunters, those who are most likely to take the initiative and be *wotshimaots,* usually sit in their own tents while other men visit them. However, the best hunters visit each other. On these visits, those present drop hints about what they want to do. Through the indirect approach of talking about the weather, the snow conditions, where different people have seen signs of caribou, and the like, one tries to sort out whom one will join on the hunt and who will be *wotshimao,* whether the *wotshimao* will travel with dogs or not, and in which direction.

Having assembled a picture of what different people in the camp want to do, each man goes back to his tent for breakfast which consists of a lot of meat and five or six mugs of tea. The atmosphere is tense and hurried while husband and wife prepare everything for the hunt. The hunter then sits down to wait while his wife keeps watch through the holes in the tent. Without warning, a *wotshimao* will dash out from the camp on his dog sled, or silently walk away on his snowshoes. The wife makes a sign to her husband who then leaves and quickly picks up the trail, and one after another, so do all the hunters who care to follow that particular leader. Others may go out hunting alone, or follow another *wotshimao.*

If the hunters are going out to shoot caribou, they usually go on foot as the dogs are a nuisance on the hunt. When they take their dog sleds, it is usually to fetch carcasses which they have shot earlier. Should they encounter caribou on the way and wish to pursue them, one or two men will stay behind with the dogs.

On snowshoes, the hunters quickly shuffle away from the camp carrying their rifles over their shoulders. The Naskapi walk at a fast and steady pace, keeping up the same speed hour after hour. When, from a hilltop, the men spot caribou (*atich*) some miles in the distance, they set off at a brisk pace alternating between putting on their snowshoes when moving in deep snow, and removing and hanging them over their rifle barrels as soon as they reach a hard and icy surface. No words are spoken. Half running, every man takes the wind, weather, and every feature of the terrain into account, and relates it to the position of the caribou. Suddenly, one of the men stops and crouches, whistling low to the other men. He has seen the herd. Without a word the men scatter in different directions. No strategy is verbalized, but each man has made up his mind about the way in which the herd can best be tackled. Seeing the other men choose their directions, he acts accordingly.

Each man approaches the animals carefully, guided by the factors mentioned above; he sees neither the other men nor the animals, and still he must act in relation to them. At the same time as he is looking out for any animal that could be standing watch, he must be wary of making any sounds. The crackling of footsteps on snowcrust travels very far, especially in cold and still weather. Once, listening to a herd of caribou passing nearly one thousand yards away, from me, I could detect those of a wolf pursuing the herd.

Finally, the hunter sees the herd. To get within shooting range, he crawls on his stomach, seeking cover behind hillocks and rocks. Contact between man and herd exists now. The animals stand nervously with their noses into the wind. They sense danger, but they cannot locate the enemy. Hopefully, the men have managed to surround the herd.

When only one, two, or three men are hunting, they often keep together. Their tactic is to shoot the lead animal as soon as the herd starts to move. If the men are well hidden and if the wind is blowing from the right direction, the herd will stop as soon as the first animal falls. Not knowing which way to go, the herd retraces its steps. Again the men shoot the first animals in the flock. If the terrain and the weather are suitable, one man alone can shoot a considerable number of animals by keeping the herd moving in a circle. The same shooting tactic is used when a larger group of men have surrounded the herd; that is, they get the herd to circulate within the pocket.

Having shot the animals they want, the men proceed to skin them at once and take out the stomachs. It is of great advantage for a man to be able to skin an animal quickly, not only because there may be many animals to do, but also because it is usually a cold task. Even warming one's hands by sticking them into the guts of the animal does not help very much since they quickly go numb again. On one occasion, the drifting snow was so thick that the men did not see a pack of wolves approach and begin eating the dead animals only a hundred yards from the hunters. In such weather, it is good to be able to skin a caribou in three minutes, as one man does. Some require as long as twenty minutes to do the job.

When the skin is off, it is folded once and laid over the carcass. If it is too late at night to skin the animals, they use their snowshoes to shovel snow over the carcasses to prevent them from freezing too much before they can fetch them with their dog sleds the following day.

The number of men that hunt together varies, not only in relation to the size of the camp, but more importantly, according to individual inclination. The Naskapi often prefer to hunt alone or with only one partner. At other times all the men in camp may go out together. There is a tendency for the latter happening when there is plenty of caribou around, whereas men hunt alone more when caribou are scarce and when there are no tracks to pursue. This they do probably for both ecological and social reasons. When caribou are scarce, the hunters have a better chance of finding them if they scatter over a wider area. Also, when meat is getting scarce in the camp, the more valuable it is and the more important and prestigious it is for a hunter to return to the camp with caribou (cf. Ridington, 1968). It is then that Luke, one of the two best hunters among the Naskapi, leaves the camp alone to shoot caribou. When meat is plentiful, the best hunters spend much time in camp giving some of the younger hunters a chance to prove themselves.

The hunting grounds of the Naskapi do not teem with caribou. The Naskapi have to search for the animals, moving their camps and hunting over a wide range of country. In their search, they use their knowledge of the country and experience with the animals and their behaviour under different circumstances. They take into account features of the terrain such as how hilly it is and whether it is forested or barren. They must consider the snow and ice conditions and relate them to the feeding and moving patterns of the caribou. They have theories about how other animals and insects such as wolves and warble flies affect the behaviour of caribou. For example, when no caribou were found in an area where it was reckoned there would be plenty, they explained this by the presence of wolves. They said that the caribou probably had fled into the forest where the deep snow cover would have kept the wolves at a distance.

They make use of this knowledge, and do not decide randomly where to search for caribou. Neither do they use the shoulder-blade divination to tell them where to look for caribou under ordinary circumstances. This is contrary to the view held by Moore (1957) who argues that the use of the shoulder-blade serves the adaptive function of randomizing the hunting of the Naskapi so that the caribou cannot learn the behaviour of the hunters. In chapter 3, I give the social explanation for the use of the shoulder-blade among the Naskapi which stresses that it was used only under circumstances of extreme uncertainty. The Naskapi never use the shoulder-blade today, although they sometimes heat one on the stove for the fun of it.

The Naskapi's knowledge of the different animals they encounter and their behaviour is extensive, and they have an acute understanding of the relationships between each species. This knowledge is accumulated through years of observation inspired by a tremendous curiosity about nature; these observations are the topic of many stories.

But they also know the behaviour of the animals and what they eat by a close association with them. Occasionally, some of the Naskapi have had wolves, bears, foxes, porcupine, and other animals living in their tents. When I first came to Davis Inlet, one man had two bear cubs living with him for several months until he had to turn them loose because they grew so big that they nearly demolished his tent and everything in it. Another man, who raised two wolf cubs, tried to put them in his dog team when they grew up but found it impossible to train them for work. Then, the man who kept a porcupine had no feeding problems with it, since the porcupine was satisfied with eating the bark off the poles inside the tent.

In the Barren Grounds, every meal consists of caribou meat. Ptarmigan, porcupine, fox, wolf, and other fauna are eaten with great relish, but more or less as snacks between meals. The Naskapi utilize almost all parts of the caribou; even the rectum is regarded as a delicacy. Meat, especially caribou meat, is considered as the only decent food and having caribou on one's scaffold is regarded as essential.

The redistribution and eating of caribou plays a significant part in the social life of the camps and strict rules guide the sharing and distribution of its various parts and hide. These rules vary with the circumstances. If two or more men are hunting together, they divide the kill equally between themselves. However, should the number of caribou and men not correspond, and should there already be enough meat in the camp, the Naskapi will not bother to quarter the animals. Without following any definite rules in this situation, the hunter who shot the most animals may get one or two animals more than the others, or a hunter with a big family may get the most while a hunter with a small family may get the least. Once back in camp, each of the hunters shares his part with the households that did not get any caribou that day. In this way, every household is assured of not only meat but also hides, as nobody can give away a caribou without giving away its skin. However, if there is little meat in the camp and the caribou has to be quartered to be shared, no skin is given away unless it is asked for. Otherwise it is important to note that meat, and usually also skins, should always be given away unsolicited. Occasionally, though, when the meat supply is running low in a camp and no caribou are shot, a family may have to inform the others when they have run out.

There is one rule which applies to any kind of animal that is shot: the man who makes the kill must always give the animal to his hunting companion. If there are several men on the hunt, the animal may be given to the oldest man in the party, to the man who stood closest to the shooter, to the leader of the hunt, or to the man who was the first to reach the carcass.

When a man is out hunting alone, he skins the animals on the spot and leaves them if the caribou are shot any distance from the camp. Back in camp, he tells each hunter to fetch his own animal or part thereof. It is common for him to designate which animal he intends for each man by telling him exactly where it lies in the terrain.

When rifle fire is heard close to the camp, any man or woman may run to the place of shooting and claim a share of the kill – even if the hunters disappear in pursuit of the herd. The men cut the throat of the caribou they want, while the women leave something behind to mark their claim. However, the people who take what they want try to assess the number of animals killed and take only their share. Later, the men fetch the caribou with dog sleds.

The meat of the animals and fish taken in traps or nets are shared in another way. The hunter himself brings the animal or fish home to his own tent where it is cooked. Then everybody in the camp goes to his tent for a communal feast. The fur of any animal taken in a trap belongs to the owner of the trap.[4] Similarly, if a group of men are fishing with hooks through the ice for red char, only the owner of the hook is allowed to control it. If a fish is caught, he brings it back to his tent where his wife cooks it, and invites as many people as possible to share it. The rest of the camp will be invited to eat the next fish caught. The fish must be eaten in the tent where it is cooked and it must be shared with others. One cannot feed it to the dogs, and the bones must not be disposed of anywhere but in the stove.

A similar rule applies to fox. The trapper himself roasts the animal in the evening and all the grown-up members of the camp come to his tent to partake in the meal. They sit in a circle around the stove enjoying the meat and the lively conversation which may go on for hours in the flickering candlelight. The bones are given back to the host who stores them safely on the scaffold outdoors. Such communal meals are very important to the Naskapi and they attend them with great fervour.

The porcupine is also shared. The hunter who brings it back to camp gives it to the first woman he meets. She, then, makes a fire to burn off the quills, quarters the animal, and cooks it. She herself or some of her children will then go about giving each household a piece of the highly prized meat. Sometimes, the pot will also be circulated in order that each household drink the broth. The hunter who brought the animal to the camp will get the head to eat.

When a porcupine is being cooked in the camp, everybody waits with great anticipation for the small piece of meat that will be his. They talk about it and the children ask each other whether or not he or she received any yet. Usually the meat is distributed when everybody is in camp, and

---

4. The Naskapi could not give me the reason for this special rule of property rights. However, it seems probable that it was developed during the period of more intense fur trapping, when the Naskapi traded with the Hudson's Bay Company.

hence everybody eats it at the same time. Although the porcupine is not eaten in one tent, the attitude towards the meat and the distribution of it make it a communal meal.

Thus, the sharing and communal eating of meat plays a significant part in the social life of the Naskapi. It is said that if some people are hungry, they must be given meat; and if they have no moccasins, they must be given skins so that they can make some and go hunting. In effect, every hunter distributes his meat and skins to all the others in camp. However, when a camp reaches the size of about eight households or more, meat and skins are given primarily to one's closer relatives. Nevertheless, if a man finds that he is the only one who has shot any caribou in the whole camp, he will share it regardless of the camp size. The result is that either all or none will be hungry in a camp.

Refusing to share meat and skins entails great social costs for an individual. Later, I shall give an example of the immediate sanctions that are applied to people who refuse to distribute their meat. But there are other sanctions operating as well. The Naskapi believe that if they break one of the rules pertaining to the handling of an animal, they will secure no more of that animal. Although they do not verbally profess to outsiders their belief in the animal spirits (in, for example, the fish spirit or *mistenaoch,* the porcupine spirit or *ohoapeio,* the fox spirit or *memekwesho*), they firmly believe that following the rules will further their relationship with the animals. Thus, the communal meals are not only a pleasant social activity and a way of sharing the meat, but they also serve to secure luck in hunting as well.

Ideally, neither meat nor skins, in fact none of the inland produce, may be bought and sold for money or be objects for barter. (However, we shall see in the following chapters that this is sometimes done.) In contrast, the store goods the Naskapi bring with them into the interior, such as tea, sugar, flour, lard, and candles may be sold and bartered. Yet, these goods, too, are given away frequently. What in fact takes place is a redistribution that leads to a levelling of supplies. It starts with people visiting one another in their spare time soon after a camp has been established, and openly examining their hosts' supply of goods. Even if the visitor's own supply is not exhausted, he can make demands on other people's goods. If he sees that his host has more of a particular item than he, he will not hesitate to ask for some of it. Consequently, within a short time every household has about the same amount of each article. Even people who are running out of an item may be asked to give it away to somebody who still has some. In the end, the original giver may have to ask the recipient for the very articles he once gave away. Therefore, every household has a special bag where it keeps a secret supply of such things as tobacco and ammunition. This bag is usually stored behind the husband's place in the tent and he is the only one allowed to open it. So that nobody sees what it contains, he opens it just enough to squeeze his hand in, and not seeing anything himself, he fumbles around for the desired object.

Thus, there is great pressure on people to share with their fellow beings. Refusing to do so, one will at once become the object of gossip – a very effective sanction in a small camp. A man who is thought of as somewhat stingy may also be tested in the following manner. A group of men are sitting in a tent. The stingy man has only one cigarette left. Another man, having a full package of cigarettes lying exposed, will suddenly ask the stingy one for his last cigarette. Everybody will turn to the stingy man watching his face intently. He can do nothing but give it away. Later, he may, of course, ask the others for tobacco.

It is clear then, that the Naskapi insist on equality with regard to consumer goods. We have seen that the distribution of meat and skins follows strict traditional rules, so heavily sanctioned that few would dare to violate them. With regard to the goods bought on the coast, however, there are no specific rules for sharing. Though people insist on sharing them when inland, this quite often gives rise to antagonism and feelings of envy. It is much more difficult to ask for a candle than for a caribou and so parents send their children to ask for store goods even though the children themselves are reluctant to do so. When people sense that a child has been sent to ask for something, they greet it with a curt "*tshekwan?*" "What is it?" (That is, "what do you want?") If the child does ask for something, the object he wants may be thrown rudely to him as he shyly waits by the door.

In fact, the Naskapi value having, as well as sharing. People often want to keep things for themselves, but it is almost impossible both to obtain and maintain a *secret* supply of anything at all, as others would at once become envious and demand sharing. One day, all the men made a trip from a hunting camp to a weather station on the Quebec border. It was decided that the anthropologist should be *wotshimao* since the purpose of the trip was to obtain, through negotiations with the white men at the station, a small supply of tea and sugar of which we had run out. In addition to tea and sugar, we got a considerable amount of flour that was too old for the white men to use, and some cereal, candies, and other items. Returning with this load, and knowing that everything would have to be portioned out carefully, I decided that it would be best to keep all the goods in their original containers until we reached camp next day as we did not have enough containers for the number of families.

Making camp that night on our way back, the atmosphere in the tent was not as pleasant as it usually is among the Naskapi. I sensed that it was caused by my decision to delay the distribution of our goods. This was confirmed by the men when I asked them about it. The next day, when the time came to divide the supplies, Luke, in whose tent I was living said to me, "I shall share out the goods since I know the Indians. Somebody is going to be mad.

It's always like that." Together, he and I measured out equal amounts of everything to each family. Luke's household, however, did not get its share. "We must always do like that," he said.

With regard to equipment and other material possessions, a Naskapi must always be prepared to lend or give away things he himself is not using at the moment. It is of little use for the owner to take extra care of his equipment since the frequent borrowers may damage it, or even lose it completely. Any compensation for damage or loss is extremely rare.

In effect, the Naskapi have a carefree attitude towards material possessions. They never put any effort into handling their equipment carefully so that it lasts longer. When they are on the move, they travel swiftly and are reluctant to waste time in ensuring their equipment against loss or damage. Sometimes they have to leave things behind on the trail to lighten the sled so that they can reach a camping place before a storm. However, to compensate for damaged or lost items they are quick to put their material goods to alternative uses. For instance, the heel of a new rubber boot may be cut off to repair a rifle, a spoon may be filed into an awl, a file or steel trap may be made into a knife, and the family's only blanket may lose a corner to replace a lost pair of mittens.

In the preceding pages, the importance of sharing and communal meals has been stressed. *Mokoshan* is also a communal meal, but it is a more elaborate and significant ritual than those described above. The Naskapi say that it is held to please the caribou spirit and to ensure future luck in hunting, especially in the hunting of caribou (see also Strong, 1929:284–285). The caribou spirit, which is called *Katipinimitaoch,* is the supreme spirit and the master of everything, including all the different animals. The ritual can be considered as an expression of the Naskapi's willingness to fulfill a transaction with the spirit.[5]

Mokoshan is held regularly throughout the winter, sometimes as often as once a week and usually on days when the weather is too bad for hunting. It is also usually held when new people arrive in camp. The ritual is a communal affair from which nobody in the camp is excluded.

---

5. This is expressed in accounts of the tent-shaking ceremony, the last of which was held by the Naskapi of Davis Inlet in 1957 when the last shaman died. My informants' accounts are summarized as follows: After the shaman (*koshabaatom*) has made a four-stick tent (*koshabassegen*), the first to enter it is *mistapeo* (a spirit). After a while, *mistapeo* asks *katipinimitaoch* (the caribou spirit) to come. And when he arrives, *mistapeo* tells him that the Indians are hungry. To this *katipinimitaoch* answers that "you are only hungry once in a while. You have been wasting the marrow-bones, therefore I am angry. You have not performed *mokoshan* in the right manner. Therefore you cannot get any food – no good hunt." To this *mistapeo* answers: "We shall try to do *mokoshan* in the right way." A whole caribou is then brought into the big tent and handled in a specific manner. *Everybody* must eat up the whole caribou. Finally *katipinimitaoch* is satisfied and all the men go out hunting – and come home with ptarmigan, fish, caribou – anything.

There are two main roles pertaining to *mokoshan*. One man is *wotshimao* of the ritual, also called *menatshitsha mokoshan* which means he who looks well after *mokoshan*. Another man is *wotshimao osken,* that is, first man of the bones. As caribou is shot and brought to the camp, every hunter brings all the long bones to the *wotshimao osken,* who then puts them on his scaffold.

Early in the morning on the day of the ritual, the wife of the *wotshimao mokoshan* tidies up the tent and lays fresh spruce branches on the floor. She takes all her children out to stay in another tent the whole day, as only men are allowed in the tent where the ritual will take place. Then the *wotshimao osken* brings all the bones from his scaffold into this tent.

When the bones have thawed out, they are divided and placed in equal piles, one for each hunter in the camp, around the stove which stands in the middle of the tent. To participate in the ritual, every boy who attends must have shot his first caribou. Once all the hunters are gathered each kneeling behind his pile of bones, they begin scraping off the meat that has been left on each bone for this purpose. This meat is then boiled.

The only fixed position in the tent is that of the *wotshimao mokoshan* who sits immediately to the left of the entrance. It is his place, however, merely because he is the owner of the tent.

The only person who does not partake in the scraping of meat is the *wotshimao osken.* He sits at the back of the tent pounding off the two ends of each clean bone that is thrown to him, with an axe or heavy mortar. He continues to crush the ends which contain marrow until they become a coarse-grained paste. To avoid wastage, canvas and skins have been hung around him to catch any bone splinters; if any fall on the floor, they are immediately picked up. Then the mass of crushed bones is put into a large kettle and when it is nearly full, they are boiled by one of the men.

There are usually enough crushed bones so that every hunter in turn can boil a kettle-full; senior men are usually the first to do this. When this "soup" has been boiled and stirred enough, the kettle is removed from the stove and the fat (*pmin*) skimmed off by each hunter and put into a smaller kettle. Extreme caution is taken so that no fat whatsoever is spilled. The spoon used for the skimming is licked clean and brushed through the man's hair before he puts it away. The kettle containing the fat is covered tightly until the next lot of fat is skimmed off and added to it.

When most of the fat has been skimmed off, snow is dropped into the kettle and stirred around until wax-like lumps of fat are formed which each hunter stores away for his family's own consumption. However, the fat must not be removed from the tent of the *mokoshan* and it is consumed there by the hunters and their families in the succeeding days. After the lumps of fat have been removed, every hunter drinks a pitcher of the remaining broth from all the kettles. The women and older children are also called in to drink the broth.

While the bone splinters have been boiling, the *wotshimao osken* has steadily been crushing the bones' ends. This may be quite a job, as it is not uncommon to use the bones of thirty caribou in the ritual – two hundred and forty bones in total. Therefore, the *wotshimao osken* often has a young man to help him. When he has prepared enough bones, he gives five or six (a few more or less, depending on how many caribou are used) to each man. The men then crack the bones open and carefully remove the raw marrow placing it on clean plates which lie on blankets or pieces of clothing spread over the floor. All the men eat the marrow together with the meat they scraped off the boiled bones. If they have any crushed dry meat, however, they prefer to mix and knead this in with the marrow.[6]

This food is handled and eaten with extreme caution. Holding his hand over the plate, with head bent forward, each man takes a small piece between his fingers and puts it in his mouth. Should a bone splinter appear in the food, it is carefully removed and put into the stove. When finished, he runs his fingers through his hair, then wipes them on a piece of cloth which is immediately thrown into the stove. All utensils used in the ritual are cleaned in a similar fashion.

After the men have finished eating, the women and children are called in to eat the marrow from the plates of their respective husbands and fathers. The mothers usually feed the children who are between five and ten years of age. Younger children are usually not allowed to participate. Again they leave as soon as they have finished.

While the men take turns boiling the bone splinters, the *wotshimao osken* starts to extract the marrow from all the bones which were not given to the men. This marrow is cut into pieces and mixed in with the skimmed fat (*pmin*). When finished, he puts the lid on the kettle and winds a lot of string around it. Finally, the kettle is wrapped up tightly in a piece of clothing and the *pmin* can be consumed months later.[7]

The whole ritual as described above often takes as long as twelve hours. The hunters are all present until the end, enjoying the perpetual conversation. As in the communal eatings described earlier in this chapter, the atmosphere is relaxed and pleasant. With regard to this aspect of the ritual, *mokoshan* seems to be set aside effectively from daily life which is not very harmonious.

---

6. This is the pemmican mentioned by several earlier authors who encountered the Naskapi. See ch. 1.

7. When the Naskapi return to Davis Inlet from the Barren Grounds, they carry with them several kettles of *pmin*. Each kettle is then usually given to the father or father-in-law of the man who received it after a *mokoshan* in the interior. If the old men in the community have already received a kettle from somebody else, they usually give their *pmin* to a brother who may also have been present in the interior. This giving away of *pmin* should be seen as a token of close social ties. The recipient of the kettle will then hold *mokoshan* in his tent or house and everybody in the community who is old enough participates in the ritual.

37

As mentioned, the Naskapi claim that they hold *mokoshan* to ensure good luck (*nemennawpawn*). To obtain this, it is of crucial importance to handle the fat and marrow in the right manner, notably without wasting any of it. To illustrate the seriousness of the ritual and of this point in particular, I shall describe two incidents. At one time, there was a mild epidemic of a stomach disease in the camp. After having eaten the food of *mokoshan*, one of the men suddenly started to vomit. He managed to get hold of a container just in time, so that no vomit was wasted but immediately thrown into the stove. In the short discussion which ensued, it was stressed how much worse the incident could have been.

At another *mokoshan*, a young boy came into the tent to eat marrow from his father's plate. The tent was crowded and the boy stepped over a big kettle of boiled bone splinters to reach his father's place. But the youngster lost his balance and one foot landed squarely in the broth. There was an instant reaction of alarm among everybody present. The boy's father, holding his son's foot over the kettle, immediately started to remove the moccasin. But it was laced tightly with leather strings and his trembling fingers could not untie them fast enough. Resolutely, the father grabbed a knife and cut the moccasin off the foot and carefully, so that not a drop fell on the floor, he threw it into the stove.

Speck (1935) describes how Indians further south on the Labrador peninsula make offerings by throwing bear fat into the fire. Among the Naskapi, the stove does not seem to serve the same ritual function today, as they do not make any offerings of fat or marrow. The throwing of bone splinters and other parts of the sacred bones into the stove seems primarily to be a safe way of disposing such material without offending the caribou spirit. However, one may of course argue that the marrow and fat of the bones are made sacred by the way they are treated. Everything connected with this food must be handled with extreme caution. Hence, a function of the stove is to "consume" parts of the sacred food which people cannot consume, such as bone splinters and pieces of cloth with fat on them. Thus, by handling and eating the food carefully and throwing what one cannot consume into the fire, the food is made sacred and effectively held apart from ordinary food.

Until thirteen years ago, the Naskapi used to dance around the stove to the sound of the drum after every *mokoshan*. But since the last shaman died, they have adhered to the missionary's teachings which say that such activities are connected with the devil. Nor have they been singing their traditional songs. (One hunter once let one of his hunting songs be recorded on tape. Nearly two years later, he listened to the recording himself and was so moved that tears appeared in his eyes – the only time I have seen an adult man shedding tears.)

Today, the Naskapi men often play checkers after *mokoshan*. It is a popular game which they play with skill and enthusiasm. All the hunters usually follow one game at a time, hanging over each other's shoulders and shouting advice to the two players, every now and then moving the bricks for them.

To sum up the main points of the chapter, it should be noted that strength, endurance, and skills are necessary in order to adapt to a nomadic life in the Barren Grounds. These values are derived from the ecological adaptation of the Naskapi to the Barrens. Letting the ecology define, to a great extent, who are losers and who are winners, the Naskapi evaluate each other's behaviour with reference to man's interaction with his environment. These values of manliness are unambiguously defined in such terms as distance travelled against the time it took, the number of animals hunted and killed under difficult conditions, blizzards grappled with, the ability to run faster than an otter and finally kill it with an axe, and so on. Because this interaction is so crucial to the Naskapi in the Barrens, their social life is filled with contexts wherein the hunters can receive immediate recognition and social rewards for their skills.

Further, we observed the tremendous emphasis placed on sharing and communal meals, indications of a basic interdependence of one Naskapi upon the other. However, this entails a fundamental dilemma in the culture: on the one hand, they must share with each other (and they do value sharing); on the other, they also value having. This contradiction points to an area of latent conflict in Naskapi society which I shall treat extensively in the ensuing chapters.

Another problem is what rights does a hunter have in the animals he kills? Surely, every household in the camp has an unquestionable right to its share of all the animals that are shot. The rules of sharing and the ritual and social sanctions enforcing these rules negate any right of the hunter to keep all the meat he shoots. But on the other hand, if giving away meat bestows prestige on a hunter, then the receivers should not have explicit rights to this meat. My data suggest that this is all kept ambiguous by the Naskapi. However, I lack conclusive evidence on this point. We should note, though, that a hunter does get prestige from his skills and performance as a hunter, as long as he also shares the meat. In the next chapter, we shall see that a hunter has good reason to share what he kills.

Leadership in the Barren Ground World

3

In the foregoing chapter, it was shown that there is a relatively equal distribution of material wealth among the Naskapi, and that social and ecological factors severely restrict the possibilities for any accumulation of wealth. Thus, there is no basis for a systematic relationship between the distribution of wealth and social rank. Although minimal equipment is required to shoot the caribou necessary to gain prestige, every Naskapi can afford to obtain it. It is possible, however, that this technological minimum will rise in the future with the introduction of, for example, motor toboggans; some Naskapi would be prevented from participating in the competition for leadership and prestige because of their inability to buy expensive equipment. There were a few Naskapi who, at the time of my field work, did not have a serviceable rifle. This, however, was due to a mismanagement of their cash – not because of a lack of cash *per se*. The following year, most of them had acquired new rifles.

Because of the limited amount of material wealth and equipment, together with their short life span, inheritance is of little importance. It is therefore safe to say that the Naskapi constitute an egalitarian society with reference to material wealth.

While store goods and most material goods may be bought and sold for money or be objects for barter, this is not so with most of the inland produce. Ideally, neither meat nor skins and skin products may circulate in this way. The general rule for the distribution of inland produce is that of common sharing.[1] By common sharing, I refer to the rules which obligate any individual who is the holder of certain goods to share them equally with any other individual, regardless of the relationship between the giver and the receiver, and regardless of whether the receiver reciprocates. That is to say, the receiver does not become obligated, through the act of receiving, to reciprocate in any manner. However, he is obligated to share with the original giver *just as he is obligated to share with everyone else* when he has anything to share. This concept of common sharing probably falls within Sahlins' category of "generalized reciprocity" (Sahlins, 1965:147).

As we saw in the foregoing chapter, there are social and ritual barriers against converting goods, that are subject to common sharing, into any

---

1. The reader should note that this discussion refers to the Barren Ground world.

41

other goods. For example, caribou meat cannot be converted into money or vice versa. I have seen a few cases (in the interior) where money was offered for caribou skins and products. In all but one case, however, the owners refused to sell or exchange. Never did I hear people *asking* for money for their skins or skin products while in the Barren Grounds, but I did hear one of the best hunters complain that he always had to give away all his skins while no one ever gave him anything.[2] His complaints, however, were mixed with overtones of pride. Later, I shall describe attempts by people to ignore the barriers against converting hunting produce into other goods.

The hunting produce which is subject to common sharing may be regarded as belonging to a separate economic sphere since its conversion into other economic goods is cut off by the same social and ritual barriers. However, if it is regarded as a separate sphere, it is important to note that conversions within this sphere are very restricted. One cannot convert skins into meat and vice versa. It is possible to exchange a skin product for another skin product and a skin for a skin product, but such exchanges rarely take place.

The goods shared in common are highly valued by the Naskapi, with caribou meat being perhaps the most central value in Naskapi culture. While not being potential economic goods (because of social and ritual barriers), they can be converted into prestige and leadership by being distributed according to the rules of common sharing. As mentioned, it is by being a skilled hunter and generous with one's meat and skins that one can gain influence and a following.

Common sharing as practised by the Naskapi has several important implications which I shall only mention here: (1) common sharing implies insurance against sickness or bad luck for any one hunter and his family; (2) this means that a hunter who brings meat and skins to the camp supplies other producers with food and clothing so that they can also contribute to the economy of the community; (3) common sharing also implies greater mobility since any individual or family may join any camp, regardless of kinship connections, and still be provided with meat. This point should be seen in relation to a fourth implication of common sharing which is the possibilities it presents for individual autonomy.

Autonomy is best seen in relation to influence where a gain in A's influence over B implies a concomitant loss of B's autonomy. But since the Naskapi household is so mobile, B can choose to move to another camp

---

2. That a good hunter at one point in time may have more skins than other people in the camp may seem to contradict the fact that skins are subject to common sharing. However, this is explained by the fission and fusion of camps throughout the winter. A good hunter may shoot 50 caribou in a camp with only 3 families. When other families join this camp later, they will ask him for skins if they have shot only a few animals.

and thus retain his autonomy. Here he may either try to establish himself as a leader, or have a relationship with the leader and the other members of the camp which is compatible with his desire for autonomy. Again, he can choose to move on if he feels that his autonomy is unduly infringed upon. Thus, in any Naskapi camp, the best hunters may compete for prestige and influence and any one of them or any of the poorer hunters can leave the camp at any time to retain his autonomy.

Individual autonomy is highly valued by the Naskapi and the influence of one individual over another is limited. It is an egalitarian society both in an economic and political sense by its rules of common sharing and the absence of an authority structure outside of the nuclear family. Nevertheless, the Naskapi do need leaders in the Barren Grounds. But the pattern of exploitation of the natural resources is such that the cooperation of more than two families is not strictly necessary, and since, as was pointed out above, the rules of common sharing make it possible for people to part and unite as they like, it becomes difficult for one man to build up a sizeable and stable following. Although the need for or possible functions of leaders in Naskapi society are limited, good hunters are able to gain influence by economic means through the rules of common sharing; however, the influence thus gained is severely limited by these same rules.

While every Naskapi can be seen as standing in the centre of a social network, the relations he has to *specific* individuals do not imply any *specific* economic obligations except those which exist within the nuclear family. Thus, a Naskapi is not obligated to give meat to a close relative, for example, to a brother, unless that relative lives in the same camp. When he gives meat to his brother, he does so because he is obligated to share with everybody in that camp.

If we view common sharing as a specific instance of Sahlins' "generalized reciprocity," we find that (1) on the level of the Naskapi band, common sharing may be regarded as a system of redistribution where all the members in a camp simultaneously receive their share from a giver or givers, and where each individual is a potential giver in a system where he must share with *everybody*. However, it should be noted that there is no "social centre where the goods meet and then flow outwards" (Sahlins, 1965:141–42), a condition which both Polanyi and Sahlins point out as a characteristic of redistribution. Although a Naskapi camp pools its resources in the sense that every member gets his share of the meat that is brought into camp, this meat is not first collected under one hand and then redistributed. However, in the ritual of *mokoshan,* the long bones are pooled together on the scaffold belonging to the chief of the bones, who then redistributes them equally to all the hunters. This may be viewed as an act symbolizing the redistribution of meat, as well as the dependence of the Naskapi on the caribou spirit.

(2) There are no ascriptive positions in the Naskapi society such as chiefs or trading partners. The Naskapi all participate equally in common sharing where, by definition, no particular act creates a partnership.

(3) There is a certain reward in the act of giving, in that one gains prestige and influence. Although the Naskapi give away meat and skins because they are obligated to do so through the rules of common sharing, they stand to gain prestige in doing so. Hence, to counter the prestige and influence which a *particular* hunter has gained through the act of sharing, it becomes necessary for his competitors to hunt and give away meat. However, the opportunities for one man to manipulate the social network by economic means are still severely limited. To make the last statement clearer, it might be useful to make a brief comparison with the Big Man in Melanesia.

He too can be seen as standing in the centre of a social network. But in contrast to the Naskapi who is immersed in a system of common sharing, the Big Man is involved in a system of balanced reciprocity. In addition, he is able to engage in trade and barter to obtain the goods he needs for converting into prestige. He can make conversions between perishable goods such as pigs and vegetables, and imperishable goods such as shell money. Thus, the Big Man is able to manipulate the social network to gain control over other people's labour and wealth. By strategically lending out goods to people who then become obligated to reciprocate, he is able to build up a great amount of outstanding credit which he can claim when he wants to perform a feast of merit, and thus convert the wealth into prestige. One can say that the most important expertise of the Big Man is his ability to manipulate his social relations and the social network.

While the crucial skill of the Big Man is manipulating his social environment, the most important for a Naskapi is manipulating his natural environment. For him, there are no ways of controlling other people's labour and converting it into prestige and influence. But there is a great difference between men in their ability to hunt, travel, and live in the Barren Grounds. Some Naskapi feel ambivalent towards the Barren Grounds; they fear not only starvation, but also the cold and blizzards and all the toil involved. Even with a store available on the coast, and the possibility of getting an aeroplane into the Barrens, it is still a risky venture to travel into the interior with one's family. It is easy to understand then, that the poorer hunters attach themselves to the better hunters who have proven their ability to travel and live in the Barrens. However, this also, is a source of ambivalence (see p. 46 ff).

The influence which a good hunter can exert over his fellows is therefore based upon the fact that he can offer them meat and safety in the Barren Grounds in exchange for which the poorer hunters are willing to relinquish some of their autonomy. It is the good hunter who takes the initiative for hunting trips and the moving of camps; the poorer hunters wait until they can join a good hunter. Early in the fall, the two best hunters travel alone into the Barrens while the others finish off the cod fishery. They are certain that they will be joined by the majority of the Naskapi who, in turn, know that if there are caribou in the Barrens, these two men will have plenty on their scaffolds. This knowledge makes it relatively safe to travel inland.

Thus, the influence which the best hunters can exert over their followers consists in taking the initiative in communal tasks. However, this influence is very limited, as they have no means whereby they can coerce people to follow them. Even after providing their followers with meat and skins for a length of time, they cannot stop them (the followers) from moving onto other camps whenever they wish to.

To be able to travel where and whenever one likes, one must have a wife since at least two people are required for driving the sled and making the camp. Even more important, somebody must stay in camp to keep the tent warm and have meat and tea ready for the hunter when he comes home at night. Hence, when only men are in the camp, one man always stays behind. In short, to attain the self-sufficiency and independence characteristic of the Naskapi, one must be married. Only then can one travel away from all other men if one wishes to. Consequently, young men in their late teens are eager to marry and establish their own households. Then they can be independent of their fathers, travel where they like, and have the right to dispose of the meat they shoot.

Both verbally and behaviourally, the Naskapi emphasize the equality and independence of all men. No one will either give or take orders from others. This does not hold true for the nuclear family, however, where the members may ask each other for various services. I can cite only one instance of a man giving orders to another outside his family. They were orders given to a man who had left his own family at the coast to travel with another into the Barrens. He was often asked to fetch wood and water, or the caribou killed by the head of the household. Thus, without his wife, he lost much of his autonomy.

The Naskapi do not tolerate any meddling from others in their decision-making. They are even reluctant to give advice, and when consulted usually answer "*mokko tchin*"; that is, "it's up to you."

Besides securing autonomy for the individual Naskapi, the mobility and self-sufficiency of each household are also important in resolving conflicts since the people involved may simply move away from each other. The independence and self-sufficiency of every household are also relevant to one's understanding of the Naskapi adaptation to their environment (see Honigman, 1949), the social organization of their hunting camps, and their pattern of leadership.

The Naskapi word for leader is *wotshimao* which they translate as "first man." This is probably an accurate translation as the term does not necessarily imply authority. It is applied not only to Naskapi men among themselves, but also to all the storekeepers on the coast and other people visiting Davis Inlet who, they sense, are important in some way. They know there is a "big" (*meshao*) *wotshimao* living in southern Canada (the prime minister). The term is also applied to Venus as the morning star: *wotshimao wapen,* which means first in the morning. The first dog in a team may also be called *wotshimao attom.* Women, however, can never be *wotshimao* "because they always stay in the tents." *Wotshimao is really any man who takes the initiative in any given situation.* What concerns us here is the man who becomes *wotshimao* when he takes the initiative to go on a hunting trip, to move a camp, or to lead the way when a group of men are travelling.

The Naskapi say that they must always have a *wotshimao.* If they do not have one, they cannot jointly leave or move the camp for any serious undertaking. The decision of who will be *wotshimao* may or may not be taken in good time before departure by all those who will hunt or travel together. If one has been chosen, then he will leave the camp first, whereupon everyone else follows. Sometimes no decision is made as to who will be *wotshimao,* in which case the first man to leave the camp will automatically become *wotshimao* if one or more men follow him. This, however, does not prevent another group from the same camp from setting out later with another man as their first man.

The group keeps to the trail chosen by the *wotshimao.* Even if an individual preferred to take a short-cut, he does not do so. If the *wotshimao* moves through deep snow without putting on his snowshoes, the others labour on and seldom take time to put theirs on also, even though they may curse the *wotshimao.* This behaviour can be understood if we consider the advantage of keeping together. Deviating from the tracks of the *wotshimao* implies running risks other than those of the first man, whether they be deeper snow, unsafe ice, or open water. Putting on one's snowshoes means lost time, especially if the surface became hard-packed soon after.

When there is doubt about which route to follow, or if the weather is making further progress difficult, the Naskapi usually stop to make a fire and discuss what to do over tea. The decision of the *wotshimao* is, in fact, a joint decision – the end result of the discussion.

Still, if an individual disagrees with the route, or finds that the *wotshimao* is travelling too slowly, he can set off on his own. If enough people follow him, he will become *wotshimao* himself. But to be able to do this, he must either have his wife with him, or when only men are travelling, some of them must be willing to follow him.

If the men undertake a longer trip, or if the camp is to be moved, the *wotshimao* is usually known a day or two before the departure. The man who takes the initiative to move the camp from one place to another is called *wotshimao meskau,* and his sled will be in front. If the group will be travelling for several days, he usually stays in front during the whole trip. He retains the "title" *wotshimao meskau* even if the group stays at one campsite for a week or two. However, this does not necessarily mean that he will be *wotshimao* in the morning should the men go out hunting.

Every Naskapi male is a hunter and can participate in the "competition," taking the initiative on trips and thus becoming *wotshimao.* But young men and less skilled hunters will of course have a poor chance of getting followers, while experienced and able hunters are certain to attract others.

In the process of deciding who will be *wotshimao,* there is usually (but not always) a lot of information-gathering on both the preceding evening and in the morning before one man finally leaves the camp as the leader. In the course of the incessant visiting between the tents, the men give each other vague hints about what their plans are. "Perhaps" (*put*) is the usual answer to the question of whether a man is going out hunting or not, and in what direction. Sometimes the situation is unresolved when the morning of the hunt arrives; at other times it is generally known who will go where and who will be *wotshimao.*

If nobody knows who will be *wotshimao,* a young man who is ambitious may take a chance and be the first to leave the camp. Perhaps then a few other young men will follow him, but there is also the possibility that he will have to hunt alone. However, because the Naskapi often hunt alone, this does not mean public defeat as long as he did not announce that he *intended* to be *wotshimao.*

The most reasonable and most common strategy for young men and older men who are not reputed hunters is to gather as much information as possible. If no other and no better hunter appears to be thinking of taking the initiative, one can carefully drop hints about one's intention. If several men say that perhaps they will go hunting in the same direction, the reaction is favourable and one may hope to have some followers.

I have also seen a young man being given the chance to be the first man. One morning fresh tracks of caribou were discovered on a distant hilltop. This young man at once went around in the camp, cautiously saying that he would like to go hunting. He went out as *wotshimao* and after a while, one of the two best hunters in the camp took up his trail. The caribou were spotted on a hilltop, but the young *wotshimao,* running far in front, picked up the wrong tracks and was led astray. It was the older and experienced hunter who quickly found the caribou. He shot most of them, and when the *wotshimao* finally appeared, he put his rifle away and signalled to the young man to kill the few animals left which were by then too tired to run in the deep snow. The young man remained *wotshimao* and led the way back into the camp.

There is no doubt that it is extremely meaningful for a Naskapi to be the first man. In one particular camp, the two best hunters regarded each other as equals. One morning, one of them got out of his blankets and made hasty preparations to go out hunting without giving or receiving any information about the other hunters. Just as he was ready to leave, he saw from his tent, his "equal" leaving the camp to go hunting also. He suddenly lost all haste and eagerness and instead went around the camp visiting. Nearly two hours later, he went hunting alone. It may be that he had hoped to be *wotshimao* and have his equal as one of his followers. At any rate, he did not want to be a follower of his equal.

Thus, the question of who will be *wotshimao* among equals must be solved when a camp has to move, or when the men venture out on a long trip of many days. On the other hand, the problem may be that nobody wants to be first man, as he has the hard job of breaking the trail. One also runs the risk of being called a poor *wotshimao*. Tough weather conditions may also make men hesitant about starting out, although some may exploit just such a situation to show their competence by taking the initiative to move.

The problems of *when* the camp will be moved and who will be *wotshimao* may be unresolved for a week on end, even if it is urgent to move. Such was the case in one camp where the meat supply had run low – so low that the dogs had to go hungry. The two best hunters, Frank and Luke, were in this camp. The men had been talking for a long time about leaving their families for several days to go hunting in another area, but no decision was made. One day, Frank signalled that he was willing to leave on such a trip by saying, "I have an extra tent but no extra stove."[3] At the same time, he also indicated that he was not willing to be *wotshimao* by saying that he had no stove. Had he decided to be *wotshimao,* he would have arranged for a stove beforehand. Nobody came up with a stove and no decision was made that day. Early the next morning, Luke went over to Frank's tent where they both decided that they should move with their families and that Luke should be *wotshimao*. They "sealed" the decision by drinking each other's beer in both tents. Later, Luke went over to a third man, taking a pitcher of beer, to tell him the news. That same morning, six families left the camp, going in another direction than in the one Luke planned to go. Both Luke and Frank claimed that they did not know beforehand of the departure of these families. Two days later, Luke and Frank departed with the eight other remaining families.

---

3. When the men go off on such trips, they often get a tent and a stove by having two families move together into one tent.

In any one camp, there tend to be only one or two men who are consistently *wotshimao.* These are the most experienced and skilled hunters. However, an older and reputed hunter may be challenged by a younger man, at any time. By slowly building up a reputation for skill and strength in *hunting, a* young man finally finds himself to be the most frequent initiator of action with a reputation for being a good *wotshimao.* He then finds that people visit his tent more frequently, making it a kind of centre in the camp.

To summarize briefly the main points of the preceding paragraphs, there are no jural or ascriptive barriers to leadership; all Naskapi men have equal rights to it, given a wife and ability to travel and hunt. However, leadership is enjoyed only in proportion to ability. We have also seen that the degree of influence which a *wotshimao* can exert over his followers is severely restricted. His leadership may be challenged at any stage of a venture. Thus, to retain his position, he must also be aware of deviating opinions among his followers. He must listen to them and voice his own opinion in relation to that of the others. He can, however, choose to initiate an action at any time in spite of the opinions of his followers, as in a show of force. If he retains most of his followers, he has proven his superiority. When facing rival *wotshimaots,* he must judge the chances he has of retaining or acquiring followers for himself. He might, of course, opt to be a follower himself.

Likewise, the potential followers must try to figure out who is thinking of being a *wotshimao* and what they are planning to do. The follower wants to know all the alternatives, since he is in a position to choose whom he wants to follow. Therefore, in any Naskapi camp, people are continually "spying" on each other, trying to find out what everyone is thinking of doing. Even when sitting inside their tents, they spy through a hole in the tent. (One day, Frank heard stirrings outside his tent and as there was no hole near him, he simply slit the canvas with his knife.) To guess the passerby's intention, one looks for several things: whether he has a rifle with him, and if so, does it look like he will be gone the whole day? Or, does he carry only an axe? How much wood has he cut? If he brings a substantial supply of wood to his tent, this might be an indication that he is thinking of leaving his family behind and going on a long hunting trip or to the store at Davis Inlet (which people may have been talking about for a long time).

As soon as several men, or only one influential man starts bringing in wood, or collecting the caribou he shot and hanging them on his scaffold, other men follow suit so that they will be ready to leave their families behind when the *wotshimao* suddenly sets out one morning from the camp. The redistribution of store goods, as described in chapter 2, leading to a balancing out of supplies among the camp households, has the effect of placing everyone in the same strategic position, at least with regard to some of the factors which they can control. Thus, if all the households have the same amount of goods such as tea, sugar, flour, and lard, they can *all* travel together further into the interior or to the coast, as the case may be.

It is obvious that with the high value they place on autonomy and with their system of competition for leadership, the Naskapi encounter great difficulties in arriving at mutual decisions. Each man is on his own; some are competing for leadership while others are waiting for a leader to whom they can attach themselves.

The process of decision-making is thus a difficult one for the Naskapi. One man must be the instigator of all joint actions. "We have no *wotshimao*, therefore we cannot leave," they say. Moreover, we have seen that the Naskapi may have difficulty in finding leaders. This is especially so in difficult circumstances. For instance, when a camp is running out of meat and nobody knows where to find caribou, much is at stake – perhaps not the lives of the camp members, but certainly the reputation of the hunters. If a good hunter goes out in one direction thinking he will find caribou there, he may lose prestige if he returns empty-handed, especially if other men have followed him.

Although the Naskapi no longer practise scapulimancy, it seems probable that it was in critical decision-making situations that they made use of this divination technique. Its primary function would be to externalize the decision of where to go and look for caribou. In this way, good hunters could blame a possible failure on the shoulder-blade and hence safe-guard themselves; it would then become easier to take the initiative to go hunting in critical situations. In my opinion, the use of the shoulder-blade is a device for solving dilemmas in decision-making among the Naskapi (cf. Park, 1963). As such, it serves an ecological function, also, by encouraging hunting trips in critical situations.

It is by looking at the extreme critical situations, those where starvation is a real threat, that we can learn more about the basis of the Naskapi system of competition for leadership and prestige, and indeed, of a whole syndrome of values in the Naskapi culture. As mentioned previously, a hunter can be the sole provider of not only his own household, but also of a whole camp with many families. A hunter who brings meat to a whole camp will inevitably be held in high esteem, and the point is brought home to everybody when a single hunter saves a whole camp from starvation. The Naskapi talk with admiration about such a man who is then, in a very real sense, the giver of life.

The Naskapi have strong opinions of what constitutes manliness and much of their behaviour can be seen as a competition with reference to these values, especially in leadership, hunting, and travelling. As one informant said with reference to hunting: "Everybody tries to beat everybody in shooting and giving away the most caribou. If we are several men together (out hunting) and the caribou has gone far away, we can agree to turn back (to the camp). But then I continue to hunt all the same. I shoot the caribou and come home late in the evening. I beat them then."

When only men are travelling, the competitive element is very strong. Although they keep together and seldom pass each other on the trail, the ideals of toughness and endurance can keep everybody running for fourteen hours at a stretch with only a twenty minute stop at noon. One must have a good excuse to give up this race without losing face.

The Naskapi relate stories about men with exceptional skills for living in the country: men with a record for shooting and giving away plenty of caribou, or men who could find their way through terrible blizzards, or save other people from starvation by enduring cold, hunger, and exertion. The Naskapi often discuss each other's merits with regard to strength, endurance, and fearlessness. For example, one evening we were gathered in the tent of one of two hunters who had not returned home even though it was late. We speculated about what could have happened in relation to the skills and former experiences of the missing hunters. When they did return, the men sat around listening intently to their accounts of the day. In this way, the Naskapi pick up valuable information about the environment. They, therefore, listen attentively to what a hunter has to say, whether he has shot caribou, or merely seen the tracks of a hare. At the same time, it is rewarding for the hunter to be the centre of attention. It means that the others recognize him as a man who has valuable information, and it gives him a chance to act out his experiences through a vigorous narrative.

Mokoshan is significant in understanding what it means for a Naskapi to be a *wotshimao*. It may be recalled that the man who takes the initiative to move and establish a camp in a new place is called *wotshimao meskau* (he also carries the *pmin* from the previous *mokoshan*). If the previous *wotshimao meskau* accompanied the group to the new camp site, he will be *wotshimao osken* in *mokoshan*, while the present *wotshimao meskau* will be *wotshimao* for the ritual in general. Because of this role, his tent becomes a kind of centre in the camp where all the men tend to congregate for recreation and for the gathering of information; but even more so, because the *wotshimao meskau* is usually one of the best hunters who, therefore, tends to initiate the daily hunting trips and also be among those who shoot the most caribou.

Hence, in the same ritual which emphasizes the importance to share, the most capable hunter also has a chance to display his qualities in the role as *wotshimao* for the ritual. We can therefore understand Luke who, being the first man to leave Davis Inlet in the fall along with several other families, eagerly awaited the arrival of most of the remaining Naskapi. "Everybody shall come in my tent and eat my food. I shall give meat away to everybody. I am *wotshimao. Mokoshan* shall be in my tent." When the people arrived from Davis Inlet, hungry for meat after a summer with only fish and store food, Luke distributed it to everybody and was the centre of attention in the ritual, during which he excitedly and with vivid gestures related his various hunting trips. The two other men who had hunted with him kept in the background during the whole ritual. Later, the camp moved under the leadership of another *wotshimao*. Feeling sad, Luke said: "I'm finished now. I'm going back to Davis Inlet. Somebody else will have *mokoshan*. Somebody down there," and he pointed at the tent of the new *wotshimao*. Luke stayed in the camp, however, and was the last to return to Davis Inlet in the spring.

The amount of prestige awarded to the hunter by his audience increases proportionately with the amount of meat he distributes and the size of the audience he entertains. However, as pointed out earlier, the amount of meat needed to acquire prestige varies with the total amount of food available in the area. It is important to recognize that the audience also includes the hunters' families. Although women take pride in their husbands as hunters, they admire the best hunters in the community. In the earlier days, the best hunters often had several wives, as did one of the active hunters today. The hunters want to make a favourable impression on the women, and vice versa. Thus, when the Naskapi talk about *nitomossets* (sweethearts), they say, "she is a good sweetheart because she can make everything so fine: sew moccasins, parkas ..."; or "he is a good sweetheart because he gives me everything: meat and skins, money to buy things ..." It is reasonable to suppose that good hunters had more than one wife because it indicated a constant show of his ability to hunt and provide. It also meant that the good hunters could control more labour, as the only labour a Naskapi can control is a spouse's. With the help of several wives, he could handle more skins and carry a bigger load on the trail at a time when the Naskapi did not have husky dogs.

Today, the Naskapi are not allowed to have more than one wife; but they do have sweethearts and lovers. Accusations of infidelity and adultery which people continually hurl at each other are a major source of gossip and quarrels. Both men and women are aggressive in approaching the opposite sex, although women do so in secrecy. Both sometimes openly brag about having a sweetheart. Although I do not have concrete data on this point, I feel that the hunters are competing not only with reference to manliness *in front of* the women, but that they are also competing *for* women.

Throughout this chapter, we have uncovered what seems to be an inherent dilemma in Naskapi culture. On the one hand, they stress equality, independence, and autonomy; on the other hand, they have a form of leadership whereby the poorer hunters are followers of the better hunters. Moreover, the position of these initiators of action is emphasized through the ritual of *mokoshan.*

In addition, the two best hunters (of a total of thirty-three) provide perhaps one-third to one-half of all the caribou shot in a year. Other men may take their families into the Barren Grounds without even carrying a rifle. I also found that when there were enough caribou around and an equal chance for everybody to kill, a few distinguished hunters kept a ledger of how many caribou were given to them. Conversely, it is important to return what is given to one in an effort to keep even in terms of prestige. However, a ledger was never kept between those who gave and those who nearly always received.

This ambivalence about leadership has not been resolved by the Naskapi. People want the prestige of being leaders, and leaders are needed. But, on the other hand, the desire to be autonomous pressures against being a follower. They all claim the right to participate in the competition for leadership, yet they have to accept the fact that leadership can be enjoyed only in proportion to ability. Seemingly, this dilemma is resolved insofar as the best hunters hardly encroach upon the autonomy of their followers, as was seen earlier in the chapter. In social interaction in general, the values of equality and autonomy are constantly expressed; even in a situation where one hunter constantly receives the meat he needs from another hunter, the two men interact as if they were equal in all respects, regardless of the one-way flow of meat.

However, there was one case where the dilemma in Naskapi values came to the surface and the "as if equal" creed was broken. Two families lived together in one tent 150 miles in the interior. The owner of the tent was by far the better hunter; the poor one did not even own a rifle. When the good hunter went hunting, the poor one sometimes followed with a shotgun over his shoulder, (for appearance sake) and a knife and a file. When the good hunter shot some caribou, the poor one would skin only the animals he wanted for himself. Most of the time, however, he stayed in the camp, only going out to fetch the caribou which the other hunters had shot earlier. He received most of his meat and skins from his host. In addition, he never cut any of the wood necessary to keep the tent warm. One evening, during a bout of drinking spruce beer, a confrontation arose. As quickly as the poor hunter placed a few pieces of meat around the stove for thawing, the host went out to his scaffold and brought back a leg of caribou which he placed between the stove and some of the other man's meat. Out of the quarrel that ensued, the host accused his guest of taking all and doing nothing in return. When the poorer hunter angrily shouted that he was thinking of returning to Davis Inlet, his host answered that that would suit him fine. The next morning, the poorer hunter erected his own tent in the camp, far away from his former host.

From the above example, we learn that even though the Naskapi usually manage to interact as equals, they are, nevertheless, conscious of the fact that they do have differing abilities as hunters and consequently make unequal contributions to the economy of the hunting camps. But only seldom is any direct reference made to this fact. In the above case, it was used as a sanction against the poorer hunter.

In their refusal to admit that some men are better hunters than others, the invariable reply of a man who is asked how many caribou he shot upon his return from hunting is that all men killed an equal number of animals each. Yet privately, every man keeps an exact account of how many animals he shoots and everybody has a rough idea of what the others kill.

Yet the question still remains as to why the best hunters do not make their superiority relevant in their daily interaction with others to a greater extent than they do. How do the Naskapi manage to interact as if they were equals in all respects? Several factors militate against the best hunters' imposing their superiority on the poorer ones. First of all, there are the implications of the practice of common sharing, primarily for individual autonomy. Secondly, both the leaders and the followers need each other, and if a good hunter insisted on making his superiority too obvious, the followers might simply leave him. (This, in fact, happened in the example cited above.) Thirdly, *mokoshan* and other communal meals play an important part in mediating between the ideal of equal ability and equal rights to leadership, and the fact that the practice of leadership varies directly with the skill of a hunter.

It will be recalled that in *mokoshan* (see Ch. 2), the cooperation of everyone is required in order to ensure the proper handling of the sacred marrow and long bones. *Mokoshan* must be performed in the proper manner in order to please the caribou spirit. Thus, even the best hunter is dependent upon all the other members of his camp in his relationship to the caribou spirit. It is only through common sharing and the way it is expressed through communal meals such as *mokoshan* that any man can obtain good luck in hunting. The best hunters are given social recognition in *mokoshan* by being given the roles of chief of the ritual or as chief of the bones, but their relationship to the animal spirits remains a communal one. Thus, the Naskapi blame some periods of starvation in the recent past on the last shaman. They all admit that he was a very strong man and the best hunter. But sometimes he was careless with *mokoshan* and the *pmin,* with the result that he spoiled the group's relationship with the caribou spirit, bringing them all bad luck in hunting. In effect, everybody has equal rights in the caribou, and the special luck that is bestowed on some men is obtained only through communal efforts.

The Beaver Indians represent an interesting contrast to the present day Naskapi with regard to their relations with the supernatural world. While the Naskapi compete for prestige and leadership only in the "natural" world, and have a communal relationship with the supernatural world,[4] the individual Beaver has individual relations with special animals he has met under special circumstances during his life (cf. Ridington, 1968; Rogers, 1962). These animals give power to the men who manage to come into contact with them. Thus, the competition for power and prestige among the Beaver takes place in the supernatural world as well as in the "natural" world. The competition between two men is a test of the relative powers of their totem animals.

Besides the supernatural sanctions operating to ensure the redistribution of meat among the Naskapi, we have seen other reasons why redistribution may be the optimal solution in disposing of one's meat. Taking part in all the activities of the hunt, especially those of the caribou, means that the individual is able to maximize a series of values. It is with reference to these activities that the Naskapi define the ideal role behaviour of men and also, to a certain degree, of women.

Thus, we have a system with gift-giving and redistribution which is maintained partly because culturally, there is no other profitable way to allocate one's resources. In the interior, a Naskapi has few dilemmas with regard to the allocation of his time and energy, of his meat and skins. The central values of the Naskapi are interrelated in such a manner that by pursuing the traditional hunting activities, a man can achieve most of his goals. Mythology, ritual life, hunting, the rules of sharing, leadership, and prestige are interconnected in such a way as to give a consistent frame of reference for one's choice of actions in the Barren Grounds. When we turn to the coastal life of the Naskapi, we shall see that the opportunities for alternative allocations of one's resources are more diversified, and that this cultural frame of reference no longer guides, without ambiguity, the choices of the Naskapi.

---

4. The shaman among the Naskapi helped out in communal communications with the supernatural world. Thus, he was powerful in this respect. But he remained dependent upon communal efforts for his luck in hunting and thereby also for the basis of his reputation as a shaman.

Socio-Territorial Groupings

4

In chapter 3, we have seen that much information is needed to decide where, when, and with whom to go hunting, and that the formation of hunting groups and camps, though the result of individual decisions of self-interest, is a *collective* process; that is, the actions of others are crucial to one's own decisions and to the success of one's own actions. These processes of information management and decision-making were seen in connection with competition for leadership and prestige, and with the sorting out of leaders and followers. This chapter will be concerned with other factors that are relevant to our understanding of the formation and composition of camps.

It has already been pointed out that a hunter needs a wife in order to establish his own household and obtain the autonomy required to move freely, attaching himself to the camps he or his wife wishes. Only then is the hunter fully responsible for the distribution of the game he shoots, and only then can a hunter join in the competition for leadership and prestige. In effect, unmarried men play no important part in the decision-making that precedes any major hunting trip. Thus, there are few incentives for unmarried young men to engage seriously in hunting besides that of learning the skills. Today, these men often find it more attractive to spend the winters in Davis Inlet or in North West River instead of travelling with their parents into the Barren Grounds.

The most influential decision-making unit in the process of camp formation is the married hunter. Yet later, we shall see that his wife also plays an important part in the decisions that are taken. The hunter and his wife, with or without their own or adopted children, make a household. A mother or father of a couple never join their children's household in the interior. Either they are too old and stay behind on the coast, or they have their own household with one or two adopted children, usually a daughter's child or children. Each household has its own tent, but sometimes two households put their tents together to make one big one. If they do, they still have separate scaffolds outside, and each family has its own stove. At any time, the two households can separate and erect their tents apart from one another. Clearly, the autonomy of the hunter (and hence, his decision-making) is dependent upon the autonomy of his household.

As head of a household, a hunter throws himself into the feverish political activities that take place in Davis Inlet a week or two before the great trek inland in the fall, trying to determine who will go with whom, where and when. Endless visiting takes place; a man may enter the same tent more than ten times in the course of a few hours in the evening. Although two men may make a more or less binding agreement to travel together, most men are reluctant to commit themselves. At least for an outsider, the situation seems to be one of confusion as everybody is trying to gather information while nobody wishes to give information. People tell each other that they do not know where they will travel, or that they will *perhaps* travel to such and such a place; they say that they do not know whom they will travel with and when they will leave. Moses[1] advised me how I should behave during this phase of a hunting trip: "That's me (Moses), I say nothing. Nothing to anybody. One day I go off, and then I go off with anybody."

Moses is not the only hunter who "says nothing." Once when I returned to his tent after a round of visiting, Bill came over. We sat for a long time without a word being uttered. After he left, Moses turned to me and asked if Bill had told me anything when I was in his tent.

Another case illustrates the same point. Moses wanted to go seal hunting. Bob, Charles, and Mark had all visited Moses' tent in the morning where the possibility of a seal hunt had been discussed as well as the possibility of staying overnight at the sealing site. Moses told me that everybody was going and so we packed our camping equipment to be ready. Then Moses went over to Charles' tent to make sure he was going too. He returned saying that Charles was not leaving after all. "He tells lies, that man," said Moses. Then Mark went to Moses' tent. They talked for a long time, and Moses concluded that there would be no seal hunt. He said that instead, he would go and check his trout nets (arctic char). But after a while, he went to Mark's tent and shortly after came running back, saying that we would go seal hunting but return in the evening. Mark was already on his way while Moses and I harnessed the dogs. When we left, Moses turned his head to see if anybody else was following. Nobody was.

There are always rumours in the community about who will travel with whom, where, and when. But checking these rumours, one often finds that according to them, one man will be travelling with two or three different groups and to different places. In fact, nobody knows the exact composition of a group until the morning of the departure.

---

1. The church today requires that the Naskapi have family names and that every individual receive a biblical name when he is baptized. In addition, most people are also known by a Naskapi name, usually a nickname referring to a personal characteristic or an incident in which the person played a prominent role. The names are often humorous, so that people laugh when they explain their meanings to a stranger (cf. Strong, 1929:286).

The kind of information-gathering and decision-making that precedes any hunting trip indicates that there are no permanent leaders with a predetermined following. How, then, do the Naskapi organize themselves? On what basis do people finally come together in a hunting group? Three major factors are taken into consideration: (1) environmental conditions, (2) prestige and leadership, and (3) kinship and sentiments.

As mentioned previously, travelling into the Barren Grounds from the coast entails certain risks. With a family, it takes nearly a week to reach the Barrens if the weather and snow conditions are favourable, and more than two weeks, if one becomes bogged down in bad weather. The problem is providing food for one's family and dogs. Until caribou are shot, one must live on provisions from the coast, supplemented by porcupine and ptarmigan found along the rivers. Some years, one is lucky and finds caribou close to the coast; other years one must travel far into the Barrens to encounter any animals. This uncertainty of the whereabouts of caribou plays an important part in the decision-making that precedes a trip inland.

To reduce the risks involved in taking families along, a group of hunters usually go into the interior alone to shoot a supply of caribou, and then return to the coast for their families. Almost nothing about the hunting trip is kept secret, so that knowledge of the stored meat at once spreads to every member of the band. The place of the kill turns into a base camp (since every family who moves to it will get its share of the meat) which is then used as a starting point for travelling and hunting further into the interior.

Once inland, the number of households in a camp may range between two and fifteen families. The size of the hunting camp, and its merging and splitting throughout the winter are partly determined ecologically. Although the household is the smallest autonomous unit, one household seldom stays alone for any length of time, because more than one hunter is needed as an insurance against sickness and accidents that may occur, and because of the nature of the hunt itself. Several men have a better chance of spotting and shooting more caribou than a single hunter has. Yet, with the use of rifles, the techniques of hunting pose few imperatives with regard to the number of hunters that are needed on any one hunt. Indeed, it is common for the Naskapi to hunt alone, whether it be for wolves, otters, caribou, or other animals.

The size of a camp must bear some relation to the number of hunters and the amount of caribou in the area. Ridington (1968) argues that a group of twenty to thirty people is the optimal size needed to minimize the dangers of illness and accidents. At the same time, a group of this size does not impede the necessary ease of mobility and it needs relatively few animals to survive. However, Ridington's calculations are based on a people who subsist on moose which is a solitary and relatively stationary animal. He calculates the average number of moose within a given area in relation to the number of hunters and their dependents exploiting the area.

With regard to the Naskapi, however, it is extremely difficult to calculate the optimal size of a hunting camp. First of all, the caribou is a gregarious and highly mobile animal that migrates over vast areas. One area may be totally devoid of caribou, while another may contain thousands of animals. The number of caribou in any one area can, of course, change not only from season to season (and from year to year), but also within a season. Neither the Naskapi nor the Euro-Canadian wildlife authorities know the exact total number of caribou in Northern Labrador or the migratory habits of the animals. Although the Naskapi always have an idea of where they might find caribou, they can never be certain of their whereabouts. Hence, they must be prepared to travel great distances, perhaps one hundred miles or more, without encountering caribou on their way. Yet in the winter, it is possible to reach an area where there are enough caribou to feed a group several times larger than Ridington's optimal group of twenty to thirty people, for a long time. But they can never be sure.

The common strategy in this situation, then, is for a few of the best hunters (often with their families) to travel inland in search of caribou and shoot a sizeable supply of meat. In this way, it becomes relatively safe for the Naskapi to bring their families into the Barrens, at least as far as the meat cache. In the winter of 1966–67, for example, Luke and two other hunters were the first to leave with their families. One family returned to Davis Inlet for Christmas with the news that they had plenty of meat in their camp. This took seven more hunters out to their camp, which was then moved further into the Barrens. There the hunters came across large herds of caribou. For two days, they hunted successfully and went back to Davis Inlet to fetch their families, while Luke and the other two families stayed behind.

Later, the number of households in this camp grew to seventeen with close to one hundred people, while just an hour's walk away, there was another camp consisting of five households with twenty-three members. Only late in the season, about Easter-time did these camps split up: most of the people went to Davis Inlet, while the rest established a camp 150 miles inland where they encountered huge herds of caribou.

Thus, the distribution of caribou that winter did not force people to return to Davis Inlet, but rather made it possible for them to remain in one large camp. The following winter most people returned to Davis Inlet, not taking the chance of going further into the Barrens. Similarly, in the winter of 1969–70, apparently no caribou were to be found in the Naskapi hunting territory, so that only a few hunters (without their families) travelled by motor toboggan into the Barren Grounds west of Nain where the herds were found that year.

Generally speaking, the Naskapi camps tend to break up into smaller units in times of scarcity and merge into larger camps when there are large concentrations of caribou. The duration of the camps also varies with the availability of caribou, from a few days to one or two months. There are other factors, however, influencing the decisions that determine the size and duration of camps. One is the security represented by the community of Davis Inlet where food is always available from the store and where medical attention is available through the missionary. Thus, the further one travels into the interior, the further one has to travel back to reach help in the event of sickness or starvation. A few years ago, a hunter cut the artery in his arm in a camp one hundred miles from Davis Inlet. While Luke's wife sewed the wound together with a needle and thread, two hunters travelled one day and one night and reached Davis Inlet in the morning. The missionary called upon the hospital plane stationed in North West River, and requested that the wounded hunter be picked up.[2]

In spite of the possibility of getting help into the Barren Grounds, many hunters with large families prefer to stay on the edge of the Barrens if the hunting is poor so that they can reach Davis Inlet as quickly as possible in the case of an emergency.[3]

Another factor influencing the size and the merging and splitting of hunting camps is that of leadership (and prestige). Since the system of competition and leadership has already been treated extensively, it need only to be mentioned here that the best hunters all seek to draw a following so as to secure a prestige-giving audience. The effect of this strategy is that the thirty-three households split into smaller groups when hunting in the interior. The sorting out of potential leaders and their potential followers is an important part of the decision-making that takes place in Davis Inlet before the great trek inland or before hunting expeditions from the camps. Thus, the difficulty that Moses and Bill had in communicating with each other (p. 58) reflected the difficulty they had in agreeing upon a transaction where one had to be the leader and the other the follower. Moses was the old and experienced hunter, while Bill was young and ambitious and certainly the next most capable hunter in the camp. Both wanted the other to go on the trip so as to maximize the possibility of a successful hunt, yet both aspired towards the leadership of the hunt.

---

2. Besides unfavourable weather conditions preventing planes from reaching the Naskapi in the Barrens, both the missionary and the medical authorities in North West River sometimes doubt the urgency of some requests, and refuse to send planes, as the operation is costly. These considerations have deterred the missionary from equipping the Naskapi with radio sets which would enable them to call for help from the interior.

3. This illustrates one way in which the white men in Davis Inlet have a covert influence upon hunting strategies.

Finally, in discussing the composition of hunting camps and their splitting and merging, we must consider Naskapi kinship and interpersonal sentiments. We have already seen that there are no permanent leaders or groups among the Naskapi. Adding up all the men who hunted during my two visits with the Naskapi, I found that nearly everybody had been together at one time or another as members of the same camp. This reflects the bilateral ideology of the Naskapi and the fact that there are *no corporate groups* based on kinship. Thus, a hunter can approach any other hunter for his companionship on a hunting trip, and a hunter who wishes to be a leader cannot count on his close relatives for his following. To avoid getting direct refusals, the Naskapi never ask directly if they can go along on a hunting trip or for anyone to join them. Instead, they approach each other by hinting at various plans, thereby avoiding any confrontations (see p. 48 ff).

No Naskapi is barred from membership in a hunting group because of the absence of close kinship links. As kinship is reckoned bilaterally and the community is so small, everyone is related to everyone else through consanguineal and/or affinal ties. However, although distantly related persons may camp and hunt together, there is a strong tendency for only members of the nuclear family and its in-laws to affiliate with each other. Between such male relatives as Fa-So, Br-Br, WiFa-DaHu, SiHu-WiBr, and WiSiHu-WiSiHu, there are strong emotional bonds and diffuse but compelling obligations to share store goods and equipment that are shared more reluctantly with others. Both in the community of Davis Inlet and in the larger hunting camps in the interior, there is a certain tendency for these relatives to place their tents close together.

Women also play an important role in the Naskapi social organization. Leacock (1954, 1955, 1969) has stressed a certain tendency among the Montagnais-Naskapi towards matrilocality. She says that they have been bilocal and exogamous, perhaps with a tendency towards matrilocality (1955). Since the Naskapi in Davis Inlet have been isolated for so long, there is no conclusive data determining whether they are matrilocal or patrilocal. After the various Indian bands on the Labrador Peninsula settled around trading posts and mining towns, the Naskapi may have been forced to practise endogamy to a much larger extent than they did before.

As mentioned previously, the Naskapi from Voisey's Bay and Davis Inlet merged into one band. Today, there are two "outsiders" in Davis Inlet who married into the group many years ago. One man is from Fort Chimo, the other from North West River. During my stay in Davis Inlet, there was one girl for whom there was no marriageable partner in the community. At the time I left Davis Inlet, she went to North West River to try to find a spouse.

Although I cannot make a definite statement regarding the residence pattern of the Naskapi, my data nevertheless suggest a matrifocal tendency in the social connections of the household. In the thirty-eight cases where two or three families moved together into one tent, twenty or thirty out of forty-four kinship links were through the female line while only seven were through the male. The table below shows the kinship linkages between the families who at one time or another lived together in one tent.[4] Where there are several possible linkages between two persons, I have listed the one that, through observation and questioning, appeared to be the most important.

This pattern is confirmed by the intimate relationships between close female relatives. They always visit and help each other with various chores. They are immensely fond of and concerned with each other's children.

It also seems reasonable to interpret the pattern of adoption as an expression of the relationship between close female relatives, especially that

Table 2. Kinship Linkages of Temporary Domestic Units

SiHu-WiBr	5
SiDaHu-WiMoBr	2
SiSo-MoBr	1
SiDa-MoBr	1
SiHuSiSo-MoBrWiBr	1
SiHuBr-BrWiBr	1
WiSiHu-WiSiHu	4
WiSiHuSiHuSiSo-MoBrWiBrWiSiHu	1
WiFaBrDaHu-WiFaBrDaHu	3
WiSiDaHu-WiMoSiHu	2
WiFa-DaHU	2
WiSiHuSiHu-WiBrWiSiHu	1
WiSiHuMoSiHu-WiSiSoWiSiHu	1
WiMoSiSo-MoSiDaHu	1
WiFaBrSo-FaBrDaHu	3
WiFaSiSo-MoBrDaHu	2
WiFaBrDaHuSiHuSiSo-MoBrWiBrWiFaBrDaHu	1
WiFaBrSoDaHu-WiFaFaBrDaHu	1
WiFaBr-BrDaHu	1
Br-Br	2
Br-Si	1
Fa-So	5
FaSiSo-MoBrSo	2
	—
Total Linkages Listed	44

4. 29% of the men in these cases have no male consanguines in Davis Inlet, while 71% have one or more male consanguines in the community with whom they, theoretically, could share a tent.

between mother and daughter. In four out of nine recorded adoptions, daughters had given one or more of their children to their parents; in the fifth case, a sister gave a child to her barren sister; in another, a woman adopted a child from her FaBrDa with whom she is also related in this way: SiHuBrWi-HuBrWiSi. The three exceptions to this pattern involved a couple who adopted the illegitimate child of a distant relative of the husband, and another couple who adopted two children of the husband's sister when both parents died. In the last case, I have been unable to establish any relationship as the child was born illegitimately in another community to parents who did not belong to Davis Inlet. All adopted children call their adopted parents *nomoshoom* and *nohom* meaning grandfather and grandmother, respectively.

A woman usually prefers to stay with her kin rather than her husband's. One man occasionally complained: "I'm lonely. I can never see my father or brothers. They are all in North West River. I want to go to North West River, but my wife wants to go home to Davis Inlet." It is also common for a newly married couple to spend more time with the wife's family than with anybody else.

A woman will usually let her husband know if she feels lonesome. Towards the end of a hunting trip in which one family was in the interior alone for two weeks, the wife started to complain of her loneliness. Finally, one day in the evening when the tent should have been put up after a day's travel, she simply disappeared into the woods. When her husband found her, he had to promise her that they would return to the camp where one of her married daughters was.

Another indication of the importance of women in the social organization is in the use of the term *nowitshewage*. This is a kinship term used by females for their female cross-cousins, their male cross-cousins' wives, and for their sisters-in-law. However, the term is also used by men, but then as the only Naskapi concept that is similar to the Euro-Canadian "friend." The Naskapi translate it as "he who helps me" and a man who accompanies one on a hunting trip is one's *nowitshewage*. As soon as the task-oriented cooperation is over, however, he is no longer one's *nowitshewage*.

It seems reasonable that this term, as used for "friend," is borrowed from the kinship terminology rather than vice-versa. It is then tempting to argue that its usage by men as the only term for "friend" is an extension of the warm and intimate relations between female relatives. It can also be seen as a way of stressing one's kith relationships to one's more distant affines (see below and Postscript). This notion is further supported by the fact that the men get satisfaction from their interaction with the environment while the women are confined to the camp where they must find excitement and satisfaction through interaction with the children and other women.

Moreover, in the competitive world of the hunter, the wife represents an element of stability in social relations.[5] The acts of seeking prestige and leadership and employing strategies to obtain them militate against any long-term relations or partnerships with other hunters.

The frequent reference in the literature[6] to the atomism of the northern Indian hunting bands seems to be true of the Naskapi also. However, as Leacock (1969:16) pointed out, this must not be interpreted to mean that there are no principles involved in their social organization. By saying that the Naskapi society is atomistic, I am simply referring to the constant reshuffling of hunting partners and changes in the composition of the hunting camps.

It is in the incessant visiting and the non-committal information management in the decision-making process which precedes the hunting trip that the atomism of the Naskapi society is most perceptible. The best and most experienced hunters are free and autonomous nuclei, around and between whom almost equally autonomous young and/or less capable hunters move as potential followers. The best hunters may also attach themselves to other good hunters, but then only reluctantly and for a limited period of time. Every hunter competes with all the others in their search for leadership and prestige regardless of their kinship relations. Although there are strong emotional bonds between brothers and fathers and sons, they want to be independent and autonomous as they compete with each other as hunters.

Yet, in the hunting camps a wide kinship network is activated. Blehr's concept of "kith-based action group" seems to apply here in that such a group "is based on a network of dyadic ties, i.e. on ramifying chains of obligations structured by kith relationships" (1963:274). As an illustration, in January 1968, camp A split into two camps, B and C; B later joined another camp which consisted of Moses, Greg, and Mark. The composition of the three camps is shown in figures 2, 3 and 4, below.

The kinship diagrams in figures 3 and 4 certainly show two networks of dyadic ties. This pattern of dyadic ties can be compared with the kinship terminology of the Naskapi which I found (with few exceptions) to be like that reported by Strong (1929) for the Barren Ground Band (see Postcript). Figure 5 gives the terms for cross-cousins (which are different from those used for ortho-cousins) and collateral affines. It should be noted here that *nitomoss* is translated as girlfriend/boyfriend and that the relationship has

---

5. This is contrary to Service's view of hunting bands which stresses "the importance of the solidarity of the males in hunting, sharing game, and particularly offence-defence" and a practice of patrilocality following from this (1962:67). It also lends support to his critics, especially Leacock (1969), Damas (1969a; 1969b), and Guemple (1970). In Ch. 3, we have seen that kinship is of little importance in the sharing of game.
6. See e.g. Balikci, Honigmann and others in *Human Organization,* Vol. 27, 1968, No. 3.

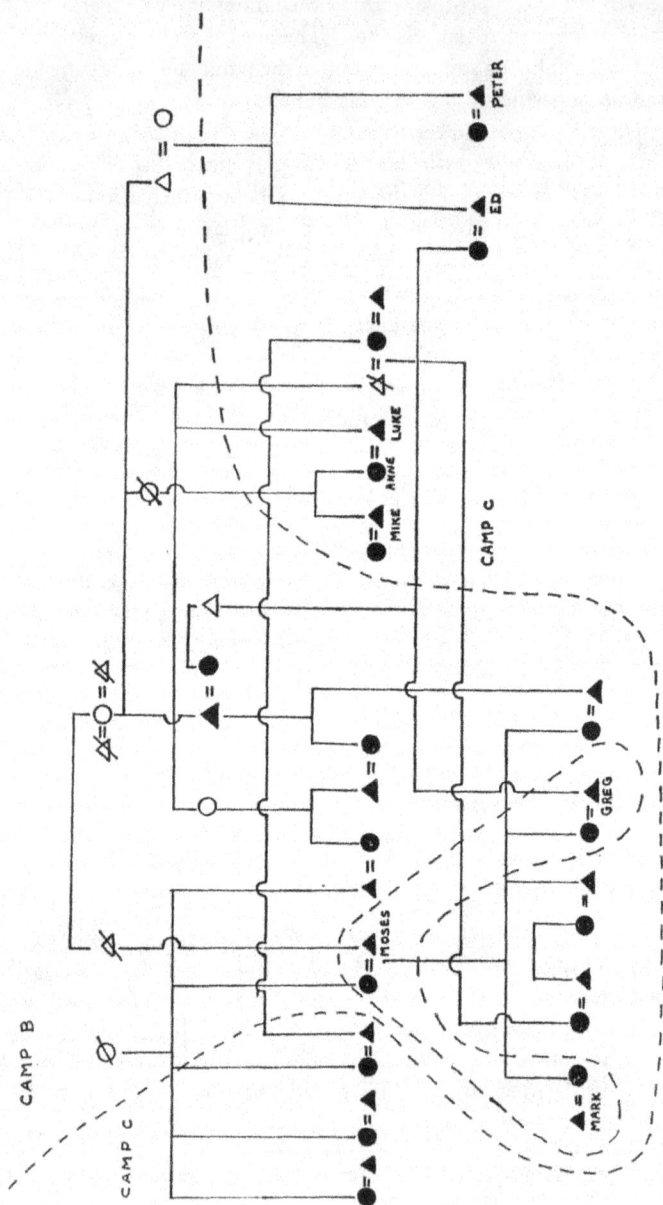

Figure 2. The Fission and Fusion of Camps

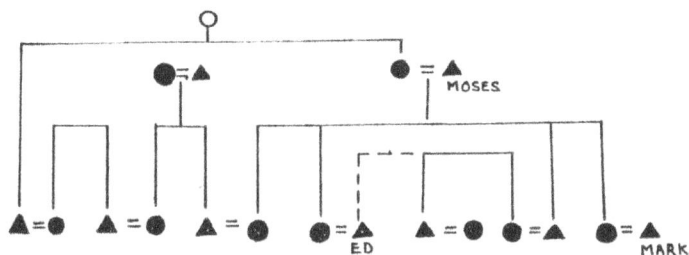

Figure 3. Kinship Composition of Camps B and D

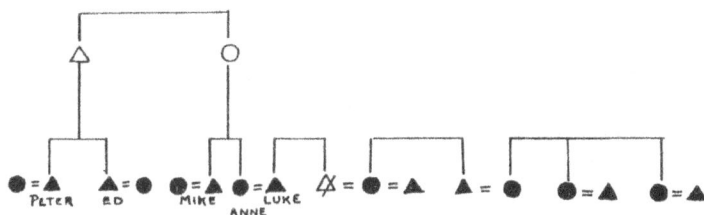

Figure 4. Kinship Composition of Camp C

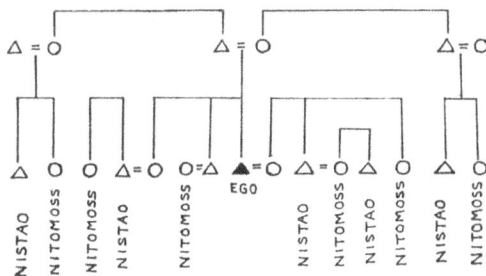

Figure 5. Kinship Terms for Cross-Cousins and Collateral Affines

obvious sexual connotations. The same term is also applied to pre- and extra-marital partners not related to ego as shown in figure 5. The term *nistao* is used with special warmth and affection (see also Honigmann, 1962:63); for example, two brothers-in-law using each other's Christian names will switch to *nistao* when they want to give each other meat, a skin, or a mug of beer. It should also be noted that the levirate and sororate are still practised. Thus, the terminological system and the Naskapi ideas about kinship seem to fit well with the proposition of kith-based action groups. Figure 5 shows clearly how a wide range of people are drawn into a kinship network which, when shown diagrammatically, forms a similar pattern to that of figures 3 and 4. In other words, the Naskapi kinship system should lend itself well as a charter for mobilizing a number of persons in a fashion similar to that described by Blehr *(ibid)*.

However, since nearly all individuals in Davis Inlet can be categorized in terms of dyadic relationships based on consanguineal and affinal ties, there is little predictive value in saying that the hunting camps are kith-based action groups. Each individual has ample opportunity, on the basis of kinship, to choose whom he wants to affiliate with. Indeed, this fact and the sharing practices which were discussed in the preceding chapters, allow for the great social (and, therefore, also physical) mobility which has been and still is very important in their ecological adaptation. Therefore, we cannot predict on the basis of kinship alone the composition of hunting camps; we are not dealing with kinship only but with (1) female companionship and (2) male partnerships and rivalries also.

It has already been shown how individual responses to ecological demands and questions of security can split a hunting camp. We have also seen how the competition for leadership and prestige influences the composition of hunting groups more or less independent of kinship relationships. Another important factor is the temporary antagonisms which can estrange the closest relatives and split existing hunting camps. The sorting out of people who can make up a congenial camp is part of the decision-making before every hunting trip. If A wants to go with B and vice versa, but B also wants to go with C who wants to go with D, then there is a problem, especially if A does not want to go with D. Such a network of friendliness and antagonism spans the whole community of Davis Inlet and includes everybody. The sorting out of compatible persons for a group is perhaps the most difficult part of the whole decision-making process.

Finally, chance factors such as the lack of dogs or other equipment may have a decisive influence and might prevent a family from following the others when they suddenly take off on a day when snow and weather conditions are favourable. A group which always leaves in a hurry is *ad hoc,* in the sense that nobody knows its exact composition until the morning it leaves. The haste with which a group leaves Davis Inlet (or sometimes a hunting camp) cannot be explained by snow and weather conditions only. A point is simply reached when the complicated and endless decision-making must come to an end. This break-off point appears abrupt as the final decision to leave is often made by a few men, sometimes just hours before leaving. Hence, many people rush to join the group when they learn about the decision. Another reason for the sudden decision of a few men to leave may be a desire to prevent more people and/or specific persons from joining the group.

Let us now return to camp A (figure 2) and look at its development, as it may make clear some of the determinants behind the establishment of hunting camps as well as their fission and fusion. A month before camp A was established, Luke, Moses, and Mike went hunting together in the interior, leaving their families on the coast. The purpose of the trip was to obtain a supply of meat before returning for their families. They shot forty-six caribou which they left on scaffolds, and then returned to Davis Inlet where knowledge about the stored meat at once spread to every member of the band. From then on, groups of families left the coast and made their way towards the meat cache.

When Luke and Mike reached the site, other families had already established a camp there. Within two weeks, all the members depicted in figure 2 joined camp A; the camp had also been visited by men who used it as a base for hunting before going back to Davis Inlet. (As it turned out, none of these men shot any caribou but they took back their share of the meat.)

Moses, who in his younger days was one of the best hunters, wanted to be leader of his own camp. Hence, he took a different route from the others together with two of his sons-in-law, Mark and Greg, and established his own camp a short hour's walk from camp A.

After nearly three weeks of blizzards and very little hunting, the supply of meat ran so low that some dogs died of hunger and people had to move. Camp A was split up (as shown in figure 2) on such a stormy day that two families turned back into the shelter of the trees and later to Davis Inlet. They excused themselves by saying that the dogs would not pull because it was too cold and blowing too hard. Later, the size of camp B was also reduced when some families with small children returned to the coast because of their fear of starvation.

The fission of "hungry" camp A is reasonable in terms of ecologic adaptation since nobody knew where the caribou were. Also, in demographic terms, an implication of such a division is that a larger population can be supported in the area since the possibility of at least one group finding caribou and surviving would be maximized. In this case, however, camp C encountered enough caribou on its way further inland to feed the whole Naskapi band. Finally, 150 miles inland, camp C stayed in an area for one month where they were surrounded by thousands of caribou the whole time.

In the spring, when camp C was moving towards the coast, it met Moses and his family who then joined camp C. For Moses and his family, this meant company and safety during the trip, and also sharing the hard work of breaking a trail further in the woods.

When the small hunting groups reach the coast, they merge into the relatively large community of Davis Inlet where it becomes impossible to observe or distinguish, by any criteria, which families have been together in hunting camps. Hunting partnerships and hunting camps are task-oriented in the sense that when the task is finished, the group dissolves and its members do not necessarily come together again to constitute another congruent group.

A hunting partnership, or the membership in a past or future hunting camp, is not kept alive as a relationship in Davis Inlet. There are no token prestations exchanged that continuously reconfirm such relationships. At any point in time, two or more men may agree to undertake a hunting trip together, but unless the decision is immediately acted upon, it will likely not be effectuated. This is as true in the coastal world as it is in the Barren Grounds.

Although all the Naskapi settle down for the summer, more or less permanently, in or around Davis Inlet, the atomism in the social life prevalent in the Barren Grounds continues on the coast. Here also, the most permanent social relations are between women, although they are frequently broken off, only to be renewed again. Some men have quite long-term relations with each other, but a conflict or dispute is always bound to arise between them that may lead to long periods of avoidance. As we have seen, interpersonal conflicts seldom arise in the interior, while disputes and conflicts play a conspicuous part in the social life of the coastal world. Although the Naskapi maximize the values of autonomy and individualism in both worlds, this individualism is coupled with interpersonal antagonism on the coast – in striking contrast to the Barren Ground world. The various reasons for this will be explored in the following chapters.

As the Naskapi move into permanent structures in the summer (tents with plywood walls, and later, houses), one might expect them to seek the opportunity to develop neighbourhoods with long-lasting social ties. To some extent, this seems to be the case. As illustrated in map 3 below, an old couple lives in house 2 with one of their married sons and his family. In tents 3, 4, and 6 live their three other sons, while in tents 1 and 12 live, their two daughters. The man in tent 7 is father of the man in tent 8 and of the wife in tent 4. The wife of the man in tent 8 is the daughter of the man in tent 3. Close kinship ties seem to play some role in the structuring of the rest of the camp also. Thus, the wife in tent 9 is sister to the man in tent 11. The wife in tent 16 is sister to the wife in tent 15. The man in tent 16 is brother of the young wife in house 2, and the man in tent 15 is brother of the man in tent 21. These two brothers have a sister in tent 14. The wife in tent 21 is a daughter of the couple in tent 12, a sister of the wife in tent 13, and a sister of the man in tent 17. The wives in tents 17 and 20 are both daughters of the couple in tent 19, while the man in tent 9 is a son of the couple. The men in tents 5 and 10 are brothers and distantly related to the old man in house 2. The wife in tent 18 is sister of the wife in tent 7. The two men in tents 10 and 16 are often hunting companions. They often stress their "affinal" relationship which they trace through the wife of the man in tent 10 who was married to a brother of the man in tent 16 until he died. They affectionately call each other by the kinship term *nistao*.

The spatial distribution of kin in the community, together with observations on interpersonal behaviour, suggest that close kinship ties play a role in the structuring of the community. Thus, the old couple in house 2 (the husband is the missionary-appointed chief in Davis Inlet) have a large family centred immediately around them, occupying tents 1, 3, 4, 6, and 8. The old couple in tent 7 belong to this "neighbourhood" because of their son in tent 8 and their daughter in tent 4.

Another neighbourhood consists of tents 13, 12, 14, 21, 15, and 16. Although the couple in tent 12 are by far the oldest in this cluster, and are parents to both the wives in tents 13 and 21 (and also to the man in tent 17), they are not the obvious centre of this neighbourhood. Rather, it is the man in tent 16 who is one of the best hunters in the community. Another focus in this cluster is the man in tent 14. This is so not only because of his wife's relatives, but also because he is a young and good hunter with a strong personality. This same man has frequent and intimate contact with the family in tent 19 where the wife is his half-sister.

The third neighbourhood consists of 17, 18, 19, and 20. The couple in tent 19 have two of their daughters living in tents 17 and 20. The man in tent 20 has no other relatives in Davis Inlet other than his wife's, and he is strongly attached to the family in tent 19. There is a latent but continuous antagonism between the man in tent 19 and the old man in tent 2. The elderly couple in tent 18 were, for various reasons, peripheral in the community, and moved to North West River in the fall of 1966.

It should be pointed out that there are more kinship connections between the people already mentioned than has been outlined above. More importantly, some close relatives of the people in this main camp were living more or less permanently (six families) in their own camp on the opposite side of the bay, on Ukasiksalik Island.[7]

Factors other than close kinship ties are involved when the Naskapi choose a place for their tent. In the case of the people on Ukasiksalik Island, their main reason for living there was their relationship with the missionary. Some were quite heavy drinkers and did not want any interference from the missionary, while others had other personal reasons for feeling antagonistic towards him. The feelings were mutual on the part of the missionary. I shall return to this aspect of community life in Davis Inlet in chapter 6.

In conclusion, it may be said that close relatives tend to cluster their tents together when they are in Davis Inlet. But these clusters do not emerge as neighbourhoods in the sense that it is "us versus those over there." There are various reasons for this: (1) the web of kinship cuts across the whole community of Davis Inlet; (2) conflicts and antagonism arise even between the closest relatives; (3) the Naskapi remain mobile, despite having plywood-wall tents and houses. Whenever they wish, they move into their cotton duck tents which they erect where and among whom they choose; (4) different individuals have different relationships with the missionary, a fact which in many ways tends to split the community in two, regardless of kinship ties; (5) but perhaps most important of all is the strong sense of individual autonomy and independence of each household that, as we have seen, allows them to move around and join hunting camps of continuously shifting membership. These last values are crucial to the cultural and social organization of the Naskapi, and are just as essential for understanding the coastal world as they are for the Barren Ground world. Strong emotional bonds between close relatives are not allowed to interfere with this autonomy.

Thus, the Naskapi do not form any corporate groups on the coast, although the possibilities are there to establish joint estates. For example, two or more men could cooperate in buying expensive equipment; but the Naskapi never do this. Just as symptomatic is their inability to form any kind of political body to deal with the white society or their representatives. Neither are they willing to surrender any of their individual autonomy to another Naskapi to act on their behalf *vis-à-vis* outsiders. These points will be considered further in later chapters.

An exception to the above is that some Naskapi get together to form two crews to operate the two cod traps in the community. However, this whole operation was instigated and led by Euro-Canadians, and the crews only function as groups with reference to the specific tasks connected with this operation.

The two men in charge of the cod traps were chosen by the missionary

---

7. Specifically: a brother of the wives in tents 15 and 16; a brother of the wife in tent 3 (he also had a married sister, now dead, living on Ukasiksalik Island, and his wife had two married sisters also living there); two brothers of the man in tent 8; a brother of the man in tent 1; and two married sisters of the wife in tent 19.

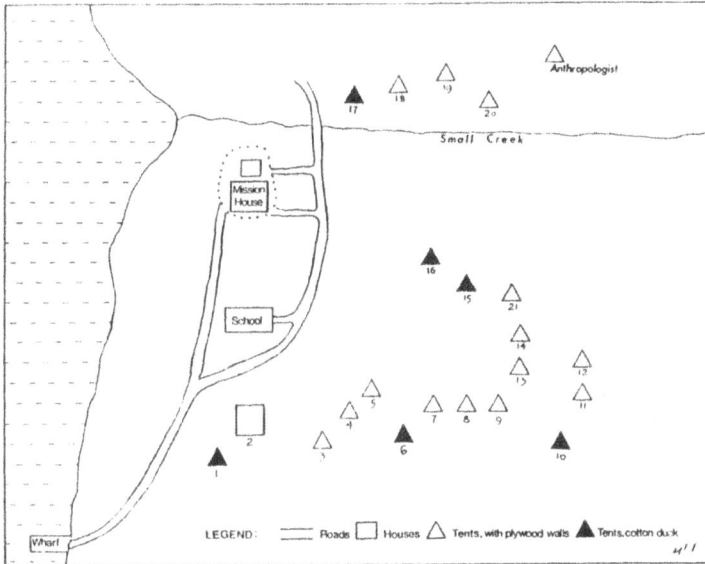

Map 3. The Old Village of Davis Inlet, July 1966

and the storekeeper mainly for their relative industriousness in economic pursuits on the coast, and because they (among others) managed to acquire large trap boats. One of them no longer drinks and is one of the men favoured by the missionary. The missionary would have liked to pick the second man from among the non-drinkers also, but reasoned that doing so would only invite hostility and trouble from those who drank and/or were opposed to him. He, therefore, chose a man who was both the most industrious and the most violently antagonistic towards the missionary.

These two men were then asked by the storekeeper to pick their own crews (see Ch. 5). This is a totally unfamiliar procedure for the Naskapi, and regrettably I was unable to observe how they went about the task. The criteria used in forming the crews are, therefore, somewhat obscure, but the different relationships with the missionary certainly were a factor. Thus, all the members in one of the crews drank and/or were opposed to the missionary, while all the members in the other crew were non-drinkers and were favoured by the missionary.

Another factor in the formation of one of the crews was that of close kinship ties. One crew consisted of the skipper's father, two of his brothers, and other non-kin, one of whom may have been chosen because he owned a trap boat. In

73

the other crew, three of the men had trap boats; another selecting factor in this crew might have been that they were all relatively industrious in their endeavours within the money economy of the coastal world. Hence, they probably expected each other to work hard and to make as much money as possible.

The membership of the two crews cuts across both the neighbourhoods outlined above and close kinship ties. In fact, neither the neighbourhoods nor the trap crews, nor the two alignments of people *vis-à-vis* the missionary represent permanent social groups among the Naskapi. The existence of permanent groups within the Naskapi society would negate the autonomy and the independence of the individual in his choice of partnerships, and ultimately also put undue constraints on when and where he could travel.

Winters 1966–67 and 1967–68
Photos by Georg Henriksen

Marie Poker with Prote Poker and their mother, Janet, in the background.

Prote Poker and George Rich.

Young girl watching over her baby brother in his cradle.

Sam Napeu: A strong and competent hunter.

Before travelling into the Barrens: Thomas Noah seal hunting *Ushtiuatshik^u* in the fall. He will use the rolled-up white screen he carries when approaching the seals at their breathing holes.

On the edge of the Barrens: The author's sled and dog team.

Families crossing *Kauinipishit namesh* to *Kauauatshikamat* where hunters had killed a number of caribou.

Mushuau Innu on the trail: A fifteen minute noon break.

Children travelling on the author's sled look towards *Kaushetinati*, the favourite hunting grounds.

A cold morning in a camp near *Ashuapun*. Temperature recorded: -65 degrees C.

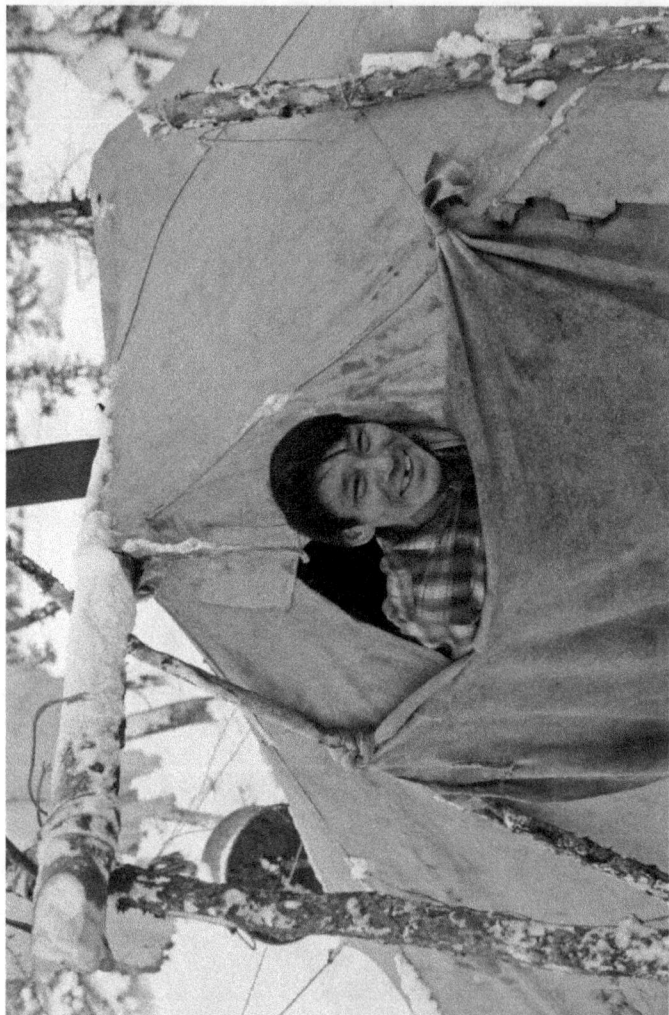

Raphael Rich keeping track of what is going on in the camp.

Sam Napeu on his way to retrieve caribou shot the day before at *Kauashetnashi.*

Ben Rich and Shipish (Elisabeth Napeu) look on while Sam Napeu skins a caribou in three and a half minutes.

Two tents are made into one, but the two families roast caribou heads on their own separate stoves. In order to have a hunter's sharp eyes, a young boy must eat one caribou eyeball.

Nabaenne (Raphael) Rich and Kaniuekutat (John Poker), following page, cut the meat off the long bones during *mukushan* (see pages 35–39 for ritual details).

Pienne Katshinak, as *wutshimau osken*, crushing the ends of the long bones during *mukushan*.

Sam Napeu and Shipish stretch and scrape a wolf skin. The caribou fetuses hanging to dry in the background are sacred food and each small bone must be carefully placed in the stove as one eats (more information page 38).

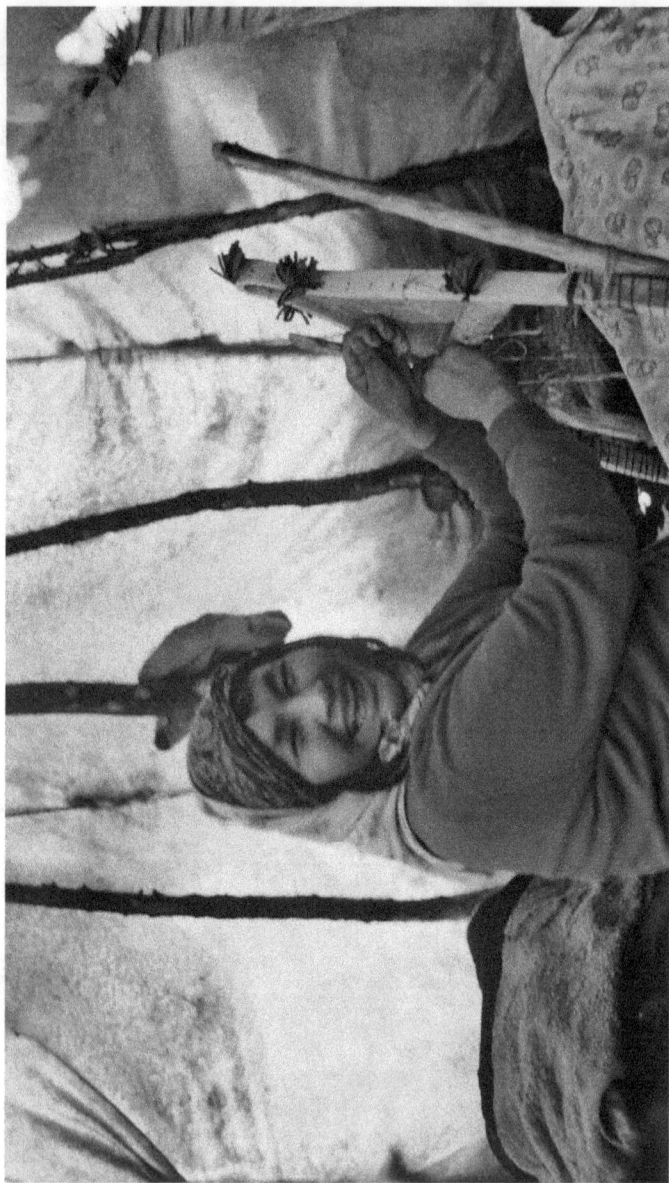

Shipish working a new pair of snowshoes. The women make the mesh in the two ends of the snowshoe, while the men mesh the middle.

Shipish and a young Johnny Piwas on the sled.

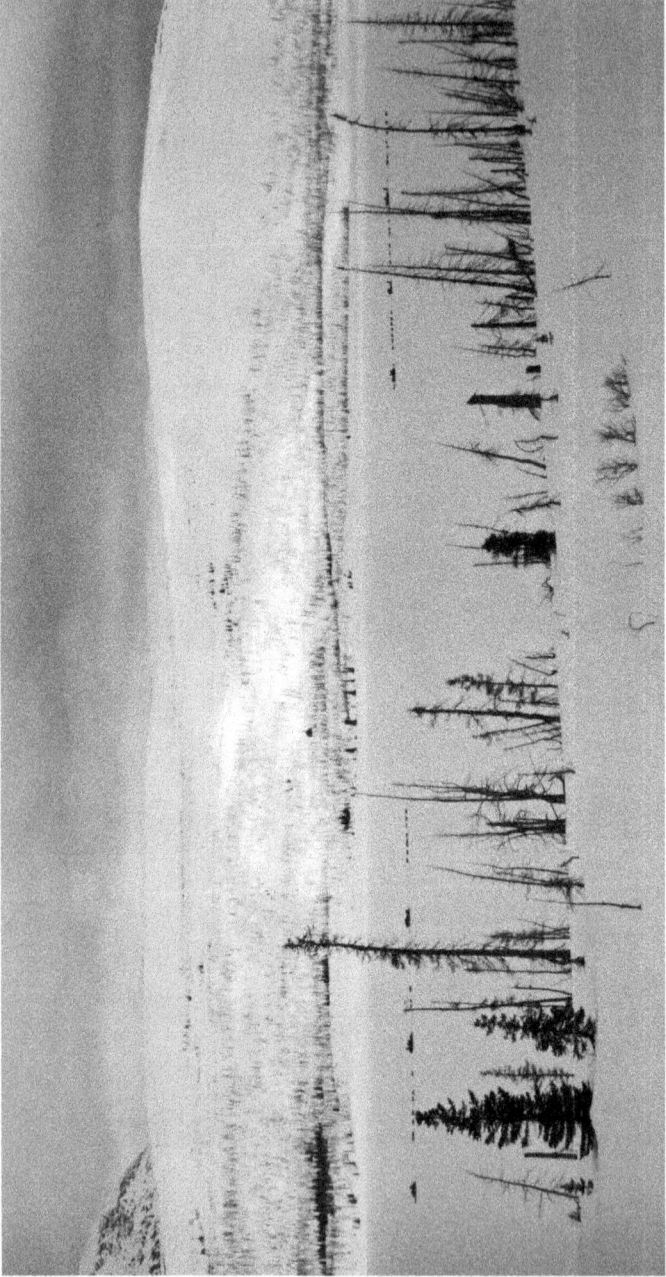

Six families travelling across *Mishti-Shuapi* on their way from the Barrens to the coast.

The old community in Davis Inlet: Thomas and Alice Noah drink tea with the author in his plywood-walled tent.

Part III: Sedentaries Under White Tutelage

The Coastal World

5

As soon as the Naskapi reach the coast and settle down in Davis Inlet for the summer, their social life and the setting in which it takes place changes in character. In the interior, it is necessary for the men to hunt to keep their families alive. In addition, the men can accumulate prestige and attain leadership, goals which spur the men to action. As will be shown, these incentives are absent on the coast; furthermore, the store is there with all its goods, and the government provides relief to those who need it, thereby securing everybody a living. Hence, although the Naskapi hunt and fish on the coast, they now can afford to relax and spend much time in their tents visiting, gambling, talking, and drinking.

In the interior, it is the hunter who brings the meat home to his family, while in Davis Inlet, it is the wife who brings home the bulk of the food from the store. There is no doubt that this conflicts with some fundamental ideas the Naskapi have regarding the role-play of men and women. We have seen the great importance which they attach to virility in the interior, and how these values are consummated in all the meat-procuring activities. Later, I shall discuss the kind of setting the coast provides for acting out proper role behaviour.

With regard to their diet, store food is much inferior to the food consumed in the Barren Grounds; it consists mainly of bread, tea, and cheap canned food. Some fresh food is acquired through hunting and fishing, but there are many days when most families subsist on only bread, tea, and tobacco. They often complain about their physical condition on the coast and usually blame the diet. Nevertheless, they also value the store food as a change in diet.

Besides hunting and fishing, there is one task performed regularly by the men throughout their whole stay in Davis Inlet, and that is fetching firewood. Living in a permanent community means that they have to travel some distance by dog sled in the winter, and by boat in the summer to get the wood they need. Every year, of course, this distance increases so that the job is quite time-consuming. The amount of wood which they get on any one trip never lasts more than a few days, so that this task may often interrupt other economic activities throughout the summer.

Snowshoes are made by the men throughout the summer and sold to the store. The two or three older men who no longer hunt in the interior, but who receive caribou skins from the younger hunters, also make them. Occasionally, a canoe is still made in Davis Inlet by splitting a huge tree into fine ribs which are then bent and shaped over steam. The hull is covered by canvas bought in the store.

Besides their usual household chores, most women occupy themselves with sewing moccasins for their families and for sale to the store. In the fall, they go out in small parties to pick blueberries, partridgeberries, and cloudberries. Once in a while, they go hunting for ptarmigan with their husbands. Like the men, they spend a lot of time visiting each other in their tents.

The children are always occupied with something in or around the village. At the age of five or six, they enter school which they attend during the parts of the fall and spring when they are in Davis Inlet. The short and sporadic attendance at school, and the inadequate supply of teachers until 1967, have meant that not one Naskapi has yet completed primary school. At the age of fifteen, children are free to leave school if they want to, and this is nearly always the case. Hence, the educational level is low; until 1968, the highest grade reached was the fifth.

While the hunting camps are marked by great congeniality, the common purpose of obtaining caribou meat, and the universal participation in communal meals, the social life in Davis Inlet is characterized by heavy drinking and many conflicts (cf. Helm, 1961), through a diversification rather than a unification of activities. There is a constant alignment and realignment of people on the basis of temporary feelings of friendship and antagonism. The most salient features of community life in Davis Inlet are the many quarrels and the incessant drinking of spruce beer in which more than half the adult male population, and some of the wives, indulge. The most frequent conflicts are caused by jealousy and accusations of adultery, and disagreements over economic transactions.

While I can explain the conflicts over economic matters (see Ch. 7), I find it difficult to explain the ever-present gossip about who is having a love affair with whom, and the troublesome effects of this gossip. It seems reasonable, however, that it is connected with the kinship system of the Naskapi, where all one's cross-cousins and siblings-in-law of the opposite sex are potential spouses. The relationship between these potential spouses is marked by sexual joking as long as the age difference is not too great. A man thirty-five years old may be seen trying to embrace a female crosscousin of eighteen amidst a lot of shouting and laughing. The girl will pretend escape while the man "battles" for physical contact. However, when a man calls a female relative of minor age *nitomoss* (according to the kinship terminology), he may tell you that it is "no good like that," meaning that it is no good to call a small girl *nitomoss*.

Strong (1929:283–84) reports a custom among the Naskapi that no longer seems to exist, at least not in any obvious observable form.

> "Among the Barren Ground people there exists a special joking relationship with sexual privileges between all men who reciprocally designate each other by the term *tcistau* (*nistao*), and between all women who call each other *nuwitciwagin* … Such men are supposed to use obscene language with each other, accompanied by much horseplay often aimed at exposure of each other's genitals … They have, moreover, the privilege of cohabiting with the other's sisters and cousins (probably only parallel cousins, but this distinction is not certain). A formal request is necessary for this privilege … Among the women the custom is limited to joking, though they go through much the same form of asking for the other's brothers. The Indians say that among the women this is only talk, whereas it actually occurs among the men. The Davis Inlet band use the same form between brothers- and sisters-in-law, and state that such exchanges do occur. As a result the terms *tcistau* and *nuwitciwagin* have a decidedly erotic association which at present makes them the centre of much amusement."

In spite of the fact that all one's cross-cousins and siblings-in-law of the opposite sex are potential spouses, I observed no sexual joking between men who call each other *nistao* or between women who call each other *nowitshewage*. Neither did I observe that they have today "the privilege of cohabiting with the other's sisters and cousins." Except for the joking relationship between relatives who call each other *nitomoss,* there seems to be very little formalism between the above categories of males and females.

In all the cases recorded of gossip and/or quarrels over love affairs, very few involved people of the categories mentioned above. This was also true of the few love affairs of which I was aware. Since gossip about love affairs is almost a daily occurrence and almost invariably leads to some degree of hostility between the accused and the accuser, it seems as if the sexual liberties once allowed in a formal manner between certain categories of relatives have become almost extinct, at the same time as people seek such liberties with others who are not members of these categories. Since such love affairs are not formalized and accepted, they lead to conflicts and hostility. However, it is hard to explain why this should be so.

One difficulty is to distinguish gossip which is based on fact from that which is not. As far as I could investigate and judge, most of the gossip circulating in the community was not based on any actual love affairs.

Rather, they were stories which people invented either to make life more interesting, or they were accusations against people with whom one had a quarrel. Whatever the origin of the quarrel, the accusations and the stories can be quite vicious. For example, once a woman accused a man of having sexual intercourse with his mother. He then accused her and her husband of killing their children (the couple once had a child who died). The woman's husband then wanted the R.C.M.P. (Royal Canadian Mounted Police) to come, but later changed his mind.

Whereas there is always gossip in Davis Inlet, there is almost none in the hunting camps in the interior. But people can foresee, while they are in the hunting camps, what events will be made the object of gossip when they reach Davis Inlet. Once, during a childbirth in a camp where all the women were present, the husband of one of the women told me, "You wait and see. When we come to Davis Inlet somebody will say that my wife was not present at the birth, and that she did not help. I know the Indians: they always tell lies."[1] There was no gossip as long as we were in the Barren Grounds, but not long after our return to Davis Inlet, the women started to accuse one another of not having been present at the birth.

It is possible that the hunting camps are too small for gossip to develop, or that people realize it would be too dangerous to let it develop. However, it seems more reasonable to suppose that the gossip starts in connection with the conflicts that are present on the coast but not in the interior (see Ch. 7), and that gossip is used as a weapon in these conflicts.

The gossip, quarrels, and conflicts are usually associated with drinking. In more than half the houses and tents in the community, a concoction of water, spruce branches, and prunes is continuously boiling; this is the brew for the beer. The beer is often drunk only a few hours after the yeast has been put in and while it is still fermenting. Only seldom do they wait more than a day before they drink it. They say that if they let the beer sit for three days, it becomes too strong. The real reason, however, is that they cannot wait that long to drink it as they do not have enough suitable containers for keeping the brew.

Those who drink, drink quite steadily. It is not unusual to see men starting to become intoxicated early in the morning, and then sleeping it off the rest of the day. Although people visit each other when they are drinking and offer each other a few mugs of beer, the typical pattern is to drink alone or with one's wife in one's own tent. There are seldom great drinking parties in Davis Inlet.

Drinking is considered evil, even by those who do not drink much. Thus, nobody drinks a mug or two of beer with a good conscience. The beer kettle

---

1. Such remarks, or similar ones, are often made by the Naskapi.

is kept more or less hidden under pieces of clothing which are removed each time a cup is refilled. When people come into the tent, some drinkers will hide their cups, also, if they contain beer. I have even seen a man who, in his hurry to hide his cup, sat on it because he could not find a better hiding place. This attitude towards alcohol has probably been created largely by the missionary who is violently opposed to any drinking by the Naskapi (see Ch. 6).

The excessive use of alcohol by some North American Indians is well known, and the Naskapi are no exception in this respect. The reasons for this pattern are far from clear, but it seems most likely that it calls for a sociological explanation. The economic behaviour in Davis Inlet probably affects the role perceptions of the two sexes. In the interior, the male is the sole provider of subsistence goods to his household, while on the coast, his economic contribution is far less conspicuous. In addition, his wife brings home a substantial portion of the household's cash income, as the family allowance cheques are issued in her name. Also, the storekeeper may insist upon issuing the goods on relief to the wife and mother of the household. Hence, the lack of role reinforcement with respect to the economic behaviour of the heads of households may be a factor behind the general unrest and heavy drinking on the coast. In a similar context, Robbins (1968) argues that the Naskapi in Schefferville obtain adequate role reinforcement through other people's positive response to their self-assertive drinking behaviour.

However, in Davis Inlet, alcohol probably plays a more significant role in people's efforts to cope with the numerous interpersonal conflicts resulting from the inconsistencies between the Barren Ground world and the coastal world. Drinking often brings on verbal attacks against others because of a disagreement over an economic transaction. A man may sit drunk in his tent, shouting out his complaints against another man, often repeating the same few sentences endlessly. If the other man concerned is within earshot, he may also sit in his tent and shout back. This kind of verbal fight is called *aienomon*.[2] Other people usually stand at a distance, listening to what is going on. Another conspicuous way of launching a verbal attack is by shouting one's complaints while staggering around in the village. Doubtless, this kind of drinking behaviour is aimed at eliciting other people's sympathy, and it is their main way of solving conflicts.

The Naskapi have only two other effective means of solving interpersonal conflicts. One way is simply to move one's tent to another place; the other is to seek support from the missionary, who is the only "court of appeal" in Davis Inlet since there is no shaman or elder with authority to intervene

---

2. I do not know how old this behaviour is. The term *aienomon* is probably derived from *aienemono* which is the term used to designate the talking of *mistapeo* in the shaking tent. *Aiemo* means talk in Naskapi. *Mistapeo* talking is also called *kankomest*.

and to judge. But as will be seen in the next chapter, the missionary is not an impartial judge. He openly admits that he always supports those who do not drink, no matter what the conflict is about and who is at fault. In spite of this, drinkers as well as non-drinkers seek his support.

The missionary has a very strong position in the community and it is strengthened by the fact that he is the "master of ceremonies" in the church. Although one can question the extent to which the Naskapi grasp and have sympathy for the teachings of the missionary, the Church is, nevertheless, important to them. There are two main reasons for this. Firstly, the Naskapi have very few ceremonials of their own in Davis Inlet, the only ritual being *mokoshan* on the odd occasion when a few caribou are brought to the community;[3] and then everybody does not always participate as there may not be enough *pmin* to go around. Thus, the Church has no serious "competition" from Naskapi ceremonials on the coast. Secondly, Holy Communion, which is by far the most important church ritual for the Naskapi, is very similar to *mokoshan*. In fact, the Naskapi say that Holy Communion is the same as *mokoshan*. This is a reasonable equation, as a comparison between the two rituals shows that they consist of similar elements: both take place within one tent/house, one man being chief of the ritual; in both, there is a small amount of sacred food that must be handled and eaten with the utmost care: in *mokoshan*, it is the raw marrow of caribou bones that is the vehicle of communication with the caribou spirit, while the bread and wine[4] unite the communicants with the body of Jesus Christ in Holy Communion.

The early accounts of *mokoshan* in the literature suggest that this similarity is not due to the Naskapi borrowing the elements of *mokoshan* from the Christian ritual. The same ritual elements are found among all the Indians on the Labrador Peninsula (see Speck, 1935), especially with regard to the bear. Similar bear rituals are also found in the old world. Rather than suggest that this similarity is a matter of diffusion, it points to the proposition that human cultures have a limited repertoire of ritual elements with which to communicate with the supernatural.

The Naskapi believe that *mokoshan* brings good luck in hunting and that the chief of *mokoshan* is a lucky man. They say that Holy Communion also is for good luck and that the missionary is a lucky man. However, they were not able to tell me what kind of luck they received, or in what matters they would be lucky

---

3. When a caribou is shot in the summer and brought to Davis Inlet, a *mokoshan skahano* is held in the community. However, at this time of year, there are not enough long bones in order for every hunter to participate in the ritual; therefore, only the oldest men in the community scrape the bones, one of them being *wotshimao mokoshan*. However, everybody participates in the eating of the *pmin,* if there is enough.

4. Only the missionary drinks the wine.

by taking part in Holy Communion. However, it seems reasonable to argue that what they are looking for is good luck in the white man's world and in their dealings with it. From the Naskapi standpoint, the missionary is obviously a lucky man as he commands the ways of the white world. Not only is he able to build a big house for himself with modern conveniences, but he can bring in aircraft and cargo with the help of his radio. I am not suggesting that the Naskapi are entirely naive with regard to these matters, but the source of the missionary's wealth remains hidden from the Naskapi. In any case, the Naskapi can see that the missionary is able to handle the white world; he has an expertise which they need. Perhaps the Naskapi consider themselves lucky, therefore, in having such a white man as chief of a white man's ritual which they equate with their own *mokoshan*.

The Naskapi desire white man's goods, but they feel the insecurity of having only limited access to them. They also show reticence and a certain amount of antagonism towards the white man who has these goods, but does not want to share them with the Naskapi. Although they do not and cannot verbalize it explicitly, they feel the intrusion upon their culture by the white man and are troubled by it. Hints of these various, yet interconnected feelings are often given out by the Naskapi. They are aware and proud of the fact that they can surpass any white man when it comes to living off the land of Labrador. They point out that they can endure cold and hunger longer than the white man, and that they do not need potatoes or flour with meat to feel satisfied. They eagerly point out that Indians do not use salt in their food (although many do so if they have any). They are proud when they contrast their tradition of sharing and helping other people with the white man's demand for money in all their undertakings. Once in a while, when new people arrived in a hunting camp in the Barren Grounds, someone would point out to me that "everybody can come here and get what he needs. It is not like that among the white men. They don't give away anything."[5]

At the same time as the Naskapi are proud of their culture and of being Indians, they are harassed by the white man and his culture and what must be a feeling of impotence in this confrontation. When the men are drunk, they may typically repeat over and over again all the things they want to buy and how much money they will pay for them. Each time, the list becomes longer and the price is doubled for each item. There can be no doubt that this reflects their inability to meet their aspirations with regard to the procurement of industrially made goods while, at the same time they realize that the white man has access to all the cash and desired goods which they lack.

Their own religious beliefs have been forced "underground" by the Church. They no longer play drums, sing, or dance, and are extremely

---

5. It is interesting to note that this is their perception of the white man and his society. The government transfer payments and other services do not alter this view, and they have no feelings of indebtedness to the white man.

reluctant to talk about their religious traditions. They do not have shamans any more and, therefore, says Joe: "Nobody knows anything about *katipinimitaoch* any more. I suppose too much Church all the time."

If they had any fear of the shamans before, they now express fear of certain white men and their possible sanctions. For example, when they have been drinking, some men often declare, in their repetitive manner, that they are not afraid either of the missionary or of the R.C.M.P. As the field of authority delegated to any white man is not clear to the Naskapi, their fear of being sanctioned is often groundless or based on misconceptions.

Quite often, rumours circulate in the community that the R.C.M.P. is coming to fetch somebody to send to jail in St. John's. Then, people who have been recently involved in a bigger (than usual) conflict, will sometimes leave Davis Inlet with their families and camp in the bush for a while. When an R.C.M.P. constable comes to Davis Inlet, he walks through the community with the missionary and/or storekeeper. Some Naskapi follow their movements from behind their tents, while others walk behind them at a distance. The atmosphere is tense in every tent, and beer kettles are hidden or even emptied. People watching white men walking through their community will make such remarks as: "now they are nicely within gunshot." Their presence is felt as an intrusion. People complain that they cannot even drink in peace within their own tents, an activity they feel should belong to the private sphere of their life. Hence, people move away from Davis Inlet from time to time during the summer to avoid the intrusions of the white man. They go into the bays so as to be able to drink without interference from the missionary. Just before I left the field, one family went into the bush because the wife was going to give birth. Had they stayed in Davis Inlet, she would have been sent to the hospital in North West River where she did not want to go.

The social life in Davis Inlet appears confused and disorganized to the observer. It is as if the Naskapi did not know what to do with their time, or as if they continuously engaged in the complex decision-making that precedes a major hunting trip, such as described in the foregoing chapter. There is a lack of any sustained co-ordinated activity, as well as any persistence in the individual's economic activities. The only notable exceptions to this tendency are (1) the cod season when some of the men fish using the two traps, and (2) since 1967, when most of the men worked quite steadily for a limited period of time each year on the preparation of the new village at Davis Inlet.

Generally, one can say that the Naskapi do not have an economic routine on the coast. They exploit the various renewable resources when they occur, but there is little sustained activity in an effort to increase the economic yield. The cod, char, and seal fisheries could be many times more intense and effective than they are today. There are several reasons for this defective adaptation to the coastal environment and the cash economy:

1. A basic characteristic of the Naskapi adaptation to their environment as hunters is the high degree of mobility of capital and labour. In order to find enough game to survive, they must always be prepared to move and to utilize whatever resources that may come their way. This kind of mobility means that they must travel with a minimum of equipment that is multi-functional. Hence, in adaptational terms, to be sedentary and to invest heavily in stationary capital equipment is contrary to Naskapi experience. By contrast, in order to exploit the coastal environment so that it yields a significant amount of cash, one must decrease one's mobility and invest in heavy equipment such as seal nets, motorboats, cod traps, and motor toboggans. It is not surprising that this change in adaptational strategy takes time for the Naskapi to adjust to.

2. The Naskapi have a limited knowledge of the coastal environment and its economic potential, and of the different techniques necessary for an effective exploitation of the resources. They also lack knowledge of the process of marketing in the outside world.

3. They lack capital equipment such as adequate boats and fishing gear, a plant for smoking arctic char and salmon, and facilities for shipping the fish fresh to southern markets.

4. The Naskapi receive government transfer payments if they are not able to produce enough for themselves. They also receive charity goods from the Church in the form of clothing. Three other factors that account for the low economic production on the coast are direct implications of Naskapi culture and society. They are the following (see Ch. 7 for further discussion):

5. The absence of the ritual, prestige, and leadership complex with regard to the exploitation of the coastal resources results in a loss of motivation in their coastal activities.

6. The lack of cooperation in economic and entrepreneurial activities by the Naskapi naturally affects production.

7. The more or less diffuse obligations to share and the defective transactions involving cash that fail to become institutionalized, represent serious restrictions for any individual seeking an effective exploitation of the coastal environment in terms of the market economy.

To illustrate these points, it is necessary to examine in more detail the economic exploitation of the coastal resources. By the time the Naskapi arrive on the coast, the seal are usually already basking in the sun, lying far out on the ice near the open sea. As the weather becomes warmer, they appear in greater numbers and closer to the shore. As long as there is firm ice, the Naskapi go out by dog sled to hunt, carrying boats on their sleds to retrieve those seals that are shot in water. However, the Naskapi seldom venture out to the edge of the ice where most of the seal are found at this time of the year. After break-up, the seal are hunted from motorboats.

The weapon used in seal hunting is the rifle, although the shotgun is used quite often when seal are hunted in the water. The most effective way to catch seal in the period between break-up and freeze-up is by the use of seal nets. However, only a few Naskapi own or use them; in the spring of 1968, the one man who used a net brought in more seal to Davis Inlet than all the men put together. This man is also the only Naskapi who owns a speedboat, which, like the motor toboggan, means much greater mobility. Mobility and speed are advantageous not only for seal hunting, but for exploiting all the resources on the coast.

Seal hunting, of course, demands certain skills. First, one must be able to stalk the animal on the ice. Crouching behind a white screen, the hunter approaches the seal whenever the animal falls asleep. It is both difficult and time-consuming to reach gunshot proximity. In addition, one must be a marksman, since the seal has to be hit either in the head or throat; no other place will do since the slightest movement of the seal's body will send it sliding through its hole in the ice into the water.

Often, the Naskapi try to stalk the seal without a screen because they have not bothered to make one. The result is that they seldom come close enough for a good shot. Moreover, some of the men have told me that they do not consider themselves good enough marksmen to hunt seal effectively.

Later in the spring when seal are hunted from boats, the animal sinks as soon as it is shot dead in the water. Thus, the Naskapi lose most of their seals during this season because they have no tool with which to retrieve them. They all say that they should make harpoons. But again, the man who used the seal net in 1968 was also the only one who made a harpoon.

There is no advantage to there being more than one or two men on a seal hunt, as one rifle shot is enough to scare the seals away from a large area. Usually, the Naskapi hunt in pairs, the man owning the sled being *wotshimao*.

The Naskapi have no rituals connected with the exploitation of the seal. However, they have one rule pertaining to its redistribution which is generally observed: the man who kills a seal must give it to the man accompanying him on the hunt. But there are no rules for further distribution when the seal is brought to the village. A man can keep the skin, meat, and fat, or he may give them to close relatives, or sell them for cash. Seal taken in nets belong to the man who put the net out.

Despite the relatively high value the Naskapi place on seal for its skin, meat, and fat, they are not very eager to hunt the animal. Whereas the settler family in Sango Bay derives the largest part of its cash income from seal, the Naskapi seldom cover their consumption needs by this means. Throughout the spring, summer, and fall, they buy meat and fat for their dogs from the settler family. Only occasionally does a Naskapi sell a seal skin to the store. In 1966, the young settler in Sango Bay earned more than $2,000 from the sale of seal skins, while the Naskapi made a mere $46.[6]

Arctic char arrives in Davis Inlet when the ice is gone, usually at the beginning of July, and it is caught in nets throughout the summer. In the autumn, when the Naskapi are camped in the bays, it is caught in nets under the ice on the frozen lakes. The catch belongs to the individual owner of the net who is free to keep it for himself, give it away, or sell it to other Naskapi for cash. There are no rules of redistribution, nor are there any rituals connected with it.

The settler family in Sango Bay catches a considerable amount of arctic char (and much less of the rare salmon) which they pickle in barrels and send to Newfoundland. This is their main economic activity during the summer. Only a few Naskapi, however, have tried to exploit this resource to obtain a cash income. The Naskapi are not encouraged by the government store to pursue this fishery for several reasons: the store would have to extend the barrels on credit and provide food on relief if no fish were caught. Furthermore, since the Naskapi would scatter to various bays to catch the salmon and char, the storekeeper would lose control over their actions. The storekeeper claims that the Indians would go hunting instead of fishing.[7]

One Naskapi has seen a new possibility of disposing of his arctic char. Being a non-drinker and a favourite of the missionary, he got permission to store his fish in the missionary's freezer. When I left the field, he expected great profits from selling the fish to people on the coastal steamer.

The main source of cash income stems from the cod fishery. Except for the two trap crews of five to six men each, the remainder of the Naskapi fish individually with jiggers. It was the missionary, using the storekeeper as a front man, who chose the two skippers; these two men, in turn, picked their own crews. However, the skippers exercise no leadership regarding the operation of the traps and receive the same number of shares as the rest of the crew. All the fishing activities are supervised by a Euro-Canadian

---

6. Some skins may have been sold to other fur companies but this amount would probably be less than $46.

7. In 1970, the government installed a small community freezer in Davis Inlet and they are now encouraging the Naskapi to fish for arctic char. N.L.S.D. has plans to build facilities for smoking the char in Nain, where they want the Naskapi to deliver their fish. This is all the more important as the declining cod fishery has been a failure for the last two years.

employed by the Newfoundland government for this purpose. It is he who decides where to put out the traps and sees that they are used properly.

The fish is salted and stored separately by the two trap crews. The men who fish with jiggers do the same. All of the fish is bought by the government and each fisherman has his own account at the store. No relief is given in the cod season. Instead, the Naskapi are given credit according to each individual's effort in catching fish. The debts are automatically paid when the government sells the fish in the autumn.

The individual's profit from the fisheries has ranged from a few dollars to $900 in a season. Members of the best trap crew earned $670 each in 1966, while $240 was the largest income among those fishing with a jigger. The two lowest incomes were $20 each. Although the type of equipment used explains the difference between the first two figures, the lowest figure can be attributed only to a lack of motivation on behalf of the fishermen. Some men do not fish for cod at all, preferring to go idle.

By fishing and by doing wage labour for the government store, the Naskapi are entitled to unemployment insurance when they obtain a certain number of "stamps." They collect stamps in numbers proportionate to the hours worked and/or the quantity of fish sold through the government. This means quite a lot of money in the winter for those who worked or caught enough fish. Not everybody seems to understand this; for example, some men may lack only one stamp to be entitled to the insurance. Even when the storekeeper tells them that they should catch a few more fish, or work another hour for the store to obtain several hundred dollars extra, they prefer not to. This may be because they do not want to be manipulated by the storekeeper.

As a cash product, cod is a scarce resource. But this is not so when it is considered as a subsistence product as everybody can easily obtain enough for consumption in season, even though the Naskapi never cure the fish for later use for themselves. Thus, there is almost no circulation of cod among them and, therefore, no rituals or rules of redistribution. The Naskapi fish it in order to earn cash or eat a dinner which, incidentally, is not highly relished.

Rock cod has no cash value, and is fished and consumed only by individual households.

Duck, geese, ptarmigan, and brook trout are usually shot and fished in such small quantities that they are consumed by the household at once. Although birds are often shared with others, they may (in Davis Inlet) also be sold for cash, even to close relatives such as a brother or a father-in-law. In any hunting camp away from Davis Inlet, however, birds are invariably shared with the others in the camp.

The black bear is valued both for its meat and skin, but plays no significant role in the economy since so few are shot each year. Although men in their late twenties can remember having seen a ritual associated with the bear similar to that of *mokoshan,* no such ceremonies are held today. The meat of a bear brought to Davis Inlet is given to close relatives of the hunter who, in turn, distribute some of their gift to others. Eventually, everybody in the community may have a taste of the bear meat. The fur may be sold for cash to a fur company, or to tourists on the coastal steamer. The meat cannot be sold for cash.

These, then, are the resources which the Naskapi exploit while they are on the coast. Let me briefly summarize the major characteristics of these economic activities: (1) Following the pattern of exploitation, the men leave the community in the morning and return the same day. They go alone, or two or three together, while their families stay at home. Different men pursue different activities at the same time; while some are hunting seals, others may be fishing brook trout in the lakes, and still others hunting geese. (2) There are very few ritual practices connected with the utilization of the coastal resources. (3) There are almost no rules for sharing game similar to the rules that apply to the animals caught in the Barren Ground world. (4) There are no effective barriers against converting the coastal resources into cash. Indeed, some of the resources are exploited for the sole purpose of obtaining cash. (5) With the new opportunities for conversion and the utilization of a wider resource base, a few Naskapi have started to become involved in individual economic pursuits, investing in capital equipment such as motorboats and motor-toboggans. (6) The Naskapi depend upon the white people in the community who play the necessary role of middleman between the Naskapi and the outside white world (see Ch. 6).

While the economy in the Barren Grounds is characterized by common sharing of most of the hunting produce, the economy on the coast is linked to the money and market economy of the white society. On the coast, the Naskapi pursue their individual economic "careers," trying, in fact, to share as little as possible with one another. Furthermore, in the Barren Grounds, the Naskapi compete for leadership and prestige, while on the coast, there are hardly any leaders and followers and almost no prestige-seeking activities. As mentioned previously, extensive rules and rituals pertaining to the game exploited are absent on the coast. The difference between the two worlds is striking, and we must ask why this is so. Why do the Naskapi not maintain the above elements of the interior world in the coastal world?

In the Barren Grounds, we find that economic production by individuals, mainly in the form of hunting, is converted into prestige and leadership; that is, the most profitable thing for a hunter to do is to share his produce with the other people in his camp. This kind of conversion, as we have seen, is sanctioned in many ways. There are social and ritual sanctions against non-sharing, as well as few opportunities to do otherwise with one's produce. Thus, to the extent that we can say that the Naskapi pursue individual "careers" of prestige and leadership in the interior world, they do so within a sharing economy. This means that the maximization of individual careers simultaneously implies the maximization of the economy and well-being of the hunting camps. There are usually no economic benefits from being a good hunter; the rewards are in the form of prestige and leadership. This situation is reversed in the coastal world where the Naskapi do pursue individual economic lives. At the same time, however, they are largely unable to gain prestige and leadership from their activities.

Between the two worlds, in fact, a barrier seems to exist. In Chapter 2, we saw how the Naskapi put pressure on each other to share the store goods as soon as they entered the interior. Yet, while birds are shared in the hunting camps, they may be sold for cash in Davis Inlet. Seemingly, traditional rules of sharing apply to European goods in the interior, while they may be disregarded with respect to some "interior" goods when these are brought to Davis Inlet. One may conclude that the barrier has to do with the *quality of life* in the interior and on the coast, and not primarily with the goods themselves. The value of goods and how they circulate is defined by the ecological and social contexts of the two worlds. Thus, one factor is the relative scarcity of goods in the two worlds, and the degree of safety and need for leadership this implies for the Naskapi. This fact may explain why the rules of sharing break down on the coast.

However, the rules pertaining to caribou meat and *pmin* do *not* change when these items are brought down to Davis Inlet. This might be because the caribou meat and *pmin* are loaded with such social and ritual values in the context of the interior world that the rules pertaining to them must be maintained in Davis Inlet. Also, as noted, they cannot be sold. (If the Barren Ground world ever became less significant to the Naskapi, the rules pertaining to the distribution of caribou would probably change. Cf. Postscript.)

It is important to note that this barrier makes difficult not only economic conversions between the two worlds, but also the attainment of prestige, influence, and leadership. Thus, the best and most influential hunters in the interior are seldom first men on the coast. In fact, the two best hunters in the interior do little else but drink in Davis Inlet, staying in their tents while the other men hunt seal and birds. Moreover, for two months they stay away from the community altogether (see Ch. 6). Yet, the prestige which the two hunters get in the interior is carried over to the coast, as manifested by the many men visiting their tents in Davis Inlet, especially during the days preceding a major hunting trip into the interior. However, this prestige is not converted into leadership in the coastal activities. The barrier between the two worlds works both ways in the sense that those men who initiate action *on the coast* and thus become first men, are not able to accumulate any prestige which can be converted into leadership *in the interior*. I believe that even if some men were able to accumulate prestige through seal hunting, for example, they would nevertheless be unable to convert this prestige into leadership in the Barren Grounds.

Being a *wotshimao* on the coast does not imply the same kind of social recognition as that of being *wotshimao* in the interior. There are several reasons for this: one is the absence of the mythological and ritual complex of the interior which makes redistribution the most reasonable way to allocate one's resources, thereby giving a hunter prestige and leadership. Another factor is the ecology of the coast – the manner in which the resources are exploited and the possibilities of displaying expertise. A third factor is the size of the community as related to the distribution of the resources. Also of importance are the economic and political roles played by the missionary and the storekeeper. Lastly, the value the Naskapi place on autonomy is of great significance and the consequent ambivalence they feel towards leadership.

Of all the economic activities on the coast, there are none that are more valued than others in terms of social recognition and prestige. In the Barren Grounds, there is no doubt that hunting caribou is the most rewarding activity, and a potential leader can always find people who are eager to go hunting. On the coast, only a few people want to do the same thing at the same time. Even when everybody is occupied with cod fishing, such an activity does not require leadership.

With the exception of the operation of the two cod traps, fishing, sealing, and bird hunting do not necessitate collective action. On the contrary, it is best to fish and hunt alone, or perhaps in pairs for reasons of safety or for the operation of big equipment such as motorboats. Thus, in exploiting the coastal resources, the Naskapi seldom establish a hunting camp where meat is distributed and leadership acknowledged. Furthermore, the man who provides the sled, motor toboggan, or boat is *wotshimao*, regardless of age, skills, or other attributes. This situation is quite different from the one in the interior, where a man who takes the initiative may find all the men following him on a caribou hunt. Hence, the opportunities to display expertise are quite different on the coast than in the interior.

In the interior, a hunter returns to a small camp where his caribou may be distributed to all the households, and where his competence and leadership are recognized in many ways, perhaps most significantly through the ritual of *mokoshan*. On the coast, a hunter returns to Davis Inlet with a few birds or seal – not enough to be distributed to all thirty-three households. In addition, he is not obliged to share with anyone at all, but may sell his produce for cash, as he does with fish, to pursue his own economic goals. Furthermore, the absence of ritual means that the Naskapi lack this important way of converting economic production into prestige, even though it also means one restriction less against conversion into cash.

Although the Naskapi accumulate capital equipment, luxury goods, and cash, it is impossible for them to convert these items into prestige. Those men who give away their cash to any extent are also the most reputed hunters in the interior. It seems as if they give away cash not because they lack prestige, but because they already have it. Many households rely on these few superior hunters when they are in the Barren Grounds, and it seems as if they want to cast them in the same role of general providers on the coast also, though without becoming their followers.

An additional factor which explains the lack of prestige connected with this new capital is that all of it is obtained from the missionary or the store. This implies that they can all acquire these goods on the same conditions. Thus, owning a motorboat is not indicative of expertise or a prestige-giving act. On the contrary, owning a motorboat means that one has fraternized with the missionary to obtain the necessary cash, behaviour which the people opposed to the missionary do not like. Considering that these people constitute more than 50 percent of the male population above the age of eighteen, it is obvious that their negative attitudes towards the missionary and those who benefit from him constitute quite an obstacle to social recognition and approval.

A significant aspect of the economic situation on the coast is that everybody has an equal chance to secure a liveable income, if not from the renewable resources, then from the social assistance provided by government transfer payments. Hence, there is no need for anybody to become a follower of good hunters. A man may accompany a good seal hunter once to obtain the skin he needs for his family's moccasins, but this is hardly enough to give the good hunter any prestige in the community. Moreover, it is more likely that the poor hunter will buy the seal skin he needs. In Davis Inlet, all the Naskapi can get what they need for the summer through the store or by buying from fellow Naskapi. When they get tired of the inferior store food, even the poorest hunters are always able to supplement their diet by hunting or fishing. Thus, the coast represents a secure environment with minimal risks for the hunter and his family. The family stays close to the store and to the missionary with his medicines, while the hunter travels within a few hours' radius of the settlement.

We noted in chapters 2 and 3 that there are two kinds of ambivalence built into the Naskapi culture: ambivalence about leadership, and about sharing. Ambivalence about leadership is based on the fact that in the interior, the poorer hunters are dependent upon the leadership of the better hunters. While leaders are needed and people want the prestige of being leaders, the value placed on autonomy pressures against being a follower.

The coastal situation, in which one need not be dependent on good hunters, provides an opportunity for casting off "followership" and enjoying autonomy. In the interior, sharing is a major mechanism for the maintenance of leadership by being generous to one's followers. But on the coast, sharing is not sufficient to maintain leadership because the "followers" are no longer in need of leaders, and the autonomy value militates against following. At the same time, since sharing does not provide the same benefits to the "sharer," there is less motivation to share. Yet, while the conversion of economic goods into prestige and leadership is impossible on the coast, new possibilities for profitable conversions have opened up through the market economy. It is profitable *not* to share, since what the Naskapi can maximize are their individual economic careers and not careers of prestige and leadership.

In the coastal world, then, the Naskapi can exercise autonomy to a greater extent than in the Barren Ground world. This seems to be the main reason for the absence of Naskapi leadership in Davis Inlet. The man who was appointed "chief" by the missionary has, in fact, no effective influence in the settlement. He is an old man who no longer takes an active part in the economic life of the Naskapi, and therefore cannot take the initiative with regard to hunting trips and other similar ventures. Neither is he a shaman who can use his supernatural powers to direct the young hunters where to go. Even if he were young and able to take initiative in hunting ventures, we have seen that the pattern of exploitation on the coast does not lend itself to the exercise of leadership and the gaining of prestige.

In chapter 6, we shall see that the "chief" does not act as a real spokesman for the Naskapi, nor as a political leader in the Naskapi's confrontation with the white man. The Naskapi have no such leader or spokesman, and they are unable to take any corporate action in their dealings with the white world. The main reason for this seems to be their insistence on retaining their individual autonomy. It is almost impossible even to gather the Naskapi for a meeting. When approached, they all answer "perhaps I come, perhaps I don't come. I am my own boss." Once at a meeting, they use their indirect approach to say things when a decision is in the making. They do not want to jeopardize their own autonomy or that of others by imposing their meaning or will on other people. Talking about another person, a Naskapi looks away from the person he is speaking to and uses technonymes. Even in their daily interaction, the Naskapi usually use the term "somebody" instead of giving a name. One has to ask whom they are talking about before they offer the name. The more information contained in what is said, the more reluctant the speaker is to reveal the identity of the person involved.

91

Thus, in order to safeguard their individual autonomy, it is impossible for the Naskapi to engage in any corporate economic or political enterprise. Neither has it been possible for any Naskapi to set himself up as a middleman and broker between the Naskapi and the white society. This is so not only because of the competition he would meet from the missionary and the storekeeper and because of the language barrier, but because of the hostility that would erupt among the Naskapi towards such an attempt by one of their own people. They would at once claim that their middleman was trying to cheat them, maximizing his own goals at the expense of others. They would feel that such a man was encroaching upon their autonomy by doing things and taking decisions on their behalf. Consequently, they would rebuff any Naskapi who tried to become a middleman between them and the white society.

Hence, the Naskapi have let themselves become clients of the missionary who, along with the storekeeper, tries to minimize the autonomy of the Naskapi. They attempt to influence the Naskapi in different ways so as to maximize their own goals: the missionary making the Naskapi into good Catholics, and the storekeeper making them into producers for the market outside. As the white men have complete control over the economic goods upon which the Naskapi depend or which they desire, they have the means by which to obligate the Naskapi to give something in return. They distribute these goods only on the condition that they get something back from the Naskapi. They want the Naskapi to relinquish their autonomy so that they can gain corresponding influence. In the next chapter, we shall see how the Naskapi approach the missionary and the storekeeper as individuals to gain personal profit, thereby making the middlemen's strategy a success.[8]

The Naskapi, themselves, do not practise common sharing with regard to the goods acquired from the white men. They now engage in economic transactions among themselves in which they have the potential means to obligate and manipulate each other. Thus, along with the opportunity to maximize individual autonomy on the coast, new possibilities are being created with the adoption of market-type transactions, to obligate and influence fellow Naskapi. I have not yet seen a Naskapi take advantage of this new opportunity to influence others. Although people with motor toboggans and motorboats are hired for transportation purposes, and are thus paid for this service, these amenities have not yet been made the basis for influence. Neither has any entrepreneurial activity taken place in which a Naskapi has managed to bind people to himself or to an enterprise. It seems

---

8. This might not be the complete answer to the strange fact that they seem to be more willing to relinquish autonomy to the white men than to other Naskapi.

impossible even for two individuals to make a joint effort towards a common economic goal involving cash. Hence, there are no Naskapi sharing investment in capital equipment. This is quite understandable from what was said above with regard to the high value the Naskapi place on autonomy.

The Naskapi situation is comparable to that of other Indian groups across Canada (see, for example, Hawthorne, 1966). We learn from them that it takes a long time before an Indian will give up any of his autonomy. This can be seen with regard to the difficulties they have in cooperating in any industrial undertaking, or in their reluctance to engage in the monotonous work of some white men under the supervision of a boss. For the same reason, they are handicapped in preparing their own leaders to deal with white men and their society.

The Naskapi and their White Patrons[1] 6

Except for the settler family who once lived in Sango Bay, it is only in Davis Inlet that the Naskapi come into contact with white men. Here they frequently interact with the missionary, the storekeeper, and since 1967, with the teacher. They also have limited contact with Eskimos and settlers from the communities of Nain and Hopedale who sometimes travel through Davis Inlet to go caribou hunting. Government officials from the Northern Labrador Services Division make brief visits to the community during the summer, and one or two politicians make an hour stop-over every election year to ask the Naskapi to vote for them.

It is crucial to our understanding of social life in Davis Inlet to know that the Naskapi are entirely dependent upon the white middlemen, notably the missionary and the storekeeper, in their economic endeavours within the money economy. The Naskapi lack the necessary knowledge of the English language to communicate with the outside world; nor do they comprehend the market economy sufficiently that they can operate on their own. They need the middlemen both for selling their own products and for the procurement of the manufactured goods they want; indeed, they need the middlemen in all their dealings with the white man's world. The Naskapi never take action as a corporate group, and there is no Indian who acts as a real spokesman for all the Naskapi.

In this chapter, I shall be concerned with the relationship between the missionary and the storekeeper, and the relationship between these two middlemen and the Naskapi.[2] By looking at the goals of these two middlemen and the strategies they adopt to gain the influence they need to achieve these goals, an understanding of how they affect community life in Davis Inlet will be arrived at. The Naskapi's relationship to these middlemen greatly affects their social life on the coast.

In this chapter I wish to bring out four points: first, that the white middlemen have to compete with *Naskapi* men of influence to gain the

---

1. The main body of this chapter also appears in R. Paine (ed.) *Patrons and Brokers in the East Arctic,* 1971.
2. The teachers are not included as they were new in the village and played no significant role in the economic and political life of the community at the time of my field work. Also, the teachers stay for only one year in Davis Inlet, a circumstance which makes it difficult for them to arrive at a position of influence.

influence they themselves desire; secondly, that the white middleman does not automatically become a leader in Davis Inlet, even though he controls vast resources. Rather, I shall argue that the middleman has to use his resources in a strategic manner to obtain influence: he has to convert his resources into influence. Should he not do so, he could find himself in a situation where the Naskapi took advantage of his resources without affording him a position of influence. Indeed, it is possible for a Naskapi to utilize the middleman's influence to gain influence for himself. We shall see that he who does gain influence is then able to initiate transactions according to his own conditions to obtain what he wants.

Thirdly, I wish to show that the struggle for power between several white middlemen of the same community (see Dunning, 1959:119) is an empirical matter relating to the assets the actors have at their disposal. Assets are "the sum total of capital, skills and social claims of an actor" (Barth, 1963:9). Assuming that no two middlemen have identical assets, this fact could well be a basis for transactions between them.

Fourthly, I intend to demonstrate, through the exposition of the strategies of the white middlemen, how they affect the social life of the Naskapi. Not only are the individual Naskapi treated differently by the middlemen, but the Naskapi themselves approach them on an individual basis to seek personal profit. The effect of the middlemen's strategies contributes significantly to the conflicts within Naskapi society – the subject of the next chapter.

I shall deal particularly with the missionary who has accumulated and now wields considerable influence in Davis Inlet in contrast to the government storekeeper. In explaining how the missionary reached and sustains his present position in the community, it is useful to analyse transactions with respect to two variables: the presence or absence of an immediate return of goods, services, or behaviour, and the range of items offered – whether they are few, or many and varied.

In many cases, the kind of transaction through which the middleman obtains influence is one where he offers a variety of goods and services and does not require an immediate return. There are at least two reasons for this. First, the middleman may initially have to create a need for any commodity he has to offer; that is, he must first give it away without asking for anything in return. Secondly, by varying the goods and services he offers (some of which his clients cannot get elsewhere), the middleman creates a general dependence upon himself. This means that subsequently, they cannot reject lightly any specific demands from him for fear of losing his favours. Were the middleman to attempt to build his influence on transactions implying immediate counter-prestations, or on transactions involving only a restricted range of items, it would be easier for the ethnic group to find alternative sources for what he offers, or simply decide that they do not need his favours.

The missionary in Davis Inlet has followed this general strategy. He is assisted in these undertakings by the fact that he is, almost by ascription, a middleman between the Indians and the white society upon which the Naskapi are already dependent, but with which they are unable to deal on their own. By the general strategy outlined above, the missionary gains so much influence in the community that his position becomes that of a patron towards the Naskapi. We should note that as a broker between the Naskapi and the white society, he seeks profit not only from the former but also from the white society; it is through a combination of the patron and broker roles that he is best able to disseminate his values to the Naskapi.

A patron is distinguished "from his client as the person who has the values of his own choosing affirmed by the others" (Paine, 1971). A broker is defined as a middleman who manipulates or processes the values which he purveys to people. A go-between conveys values faithfully without any manipulations, while a broker in his conveyance, manipulates the values involved so as to gain profit. Thus, a person may undertake acts of brokerage both to gain and maintain a position as a patron, a position in which he is seen by his clients as the source of the values that he disseminates to them (Paine, *op. cit.*).

In each of the communities in Northern Labrador, there is a store owned and operated by the Newfoundland government. The storekeeper in Davis Inlet is appointed and paid by the government and it is he who is required to execute government policy in Davis Inlet. This is, first and foremost, a welfare policy, and the storekeeper in Davis Inlet is also the welfare officer. He sees to it that nobody suffers serious want. He gives out relief, family allowance cheques, and old age pensions. However, the government also encourages the Naskapi to be self-supporting in the summer by fishing and selling cod. They are provided with small boats, cod traps, and a ready market for salt cod in Newfoundland. The storekeeper administrates the entire enterprise.

The store in Davis Inlet stocks only the most basic consumption goods, and it works on a non-profit basis. Since the storekeeper works for a fixed wage, he has little interest in increasing sales. Personally, he cannot make any economic profits from his dealings with the Naskapi. He is stationed there for a relatively short period of time, his main goal being that of saving money from his salary and working for a promotion that will give him a position in the provincial capital. His major concern is therefore to please his superiors. His superiors evaluate him according to how well he balances the accounts (the books are inspected regularly), *and how well he gets along with the Naskapi.*

The store is the only building on an island across the bay from the Naskapi camp.[3] Most of the storekeeper's contacts with the Naskapi take place over the counter in the store. His relationship with them is under constant strain because he deals with their monetary affairs, a difficult task because the Naskapi have only a limited knowledge of how goods and money are handled in the store; they do not know all the regulations the storekeeper must follow in doing his job. They often accuse him of cheating and are generally suspicious because much of the money they earn is simply recorded in the accounts. The storekeeper's problem is compounded by the fact that he has no knowledge of the Naskapi language, and hence whenever a problem arises between him and the Naskapi, both parties seek help from the missionary who lives in the middle of the Naskapi camp and speaks Naskapi fluently.

The missionary works for the Catholic Church and is answerable only to his ecclesiastical superior in Montreal. The Church does, of course, put certain restrictions on the missionary's behaviour, but his work is rarely inspected. He must submit yearly reports on his work in the community and he cannot deviate much from proper priestly decorum as there are other missionaries on the coast who would soon get to know if he did. Otherwise, he is relatively free to use what means he sees fit to make the Naskapi good Catholics. Thus, in contrast to the storekeeper, the missionary is able to use economic and technical resources strategically to obtain influence.

There are, however, certain restrictions on his behaviour which stem from his position in the community. He needs the cooperation of the storekeeper and the government, and must therefore consider this when he is dealing with them. Also, in contrast to the storekeeper, the missionary is stationed in the community for an indefinite period of time. The storekeeper has his family in Davis Inlet and knows that he will be leaving the community. The missionary is alone, and might be there to stay, and so must not do things that would prejudice his future relations with the Naskapi.

The goals towards which the missionary works are of a religious and moral nature which are essentially to make the Naskapi into "good Christians." This he cannot do by preaching only, but he must also pursue an active economic policy. He says that if life is to be "meaningful for the Indians," they must have work to do in the summer. It was originally the missionary's idea that they fish cod and he who asked the government not to give out relief in the cod season. The missionary and the storekeeper work together in trying to encourage the Naskapi to fish as much as possible. (As mentioned, the Naskapi must then trade on credit, thereby forcing them to fish.)

---

3. I refer to the old community of Davis Inlet. In the new community, the store is in the village where the storekeeper now also resides. In future, this may modify the picture I give here of the respective relationships which the two middlemen have with the Naskapi. However, if the high turn-over of storekeepers continues, the position of the missionary should not become significantly weakened.

The missionary, like the storekeeper, does not profit economically from the Naskapi. This is one of the reasons why these two middlemen are able to cooperate with one another. Another reason is that the storekeeper's economic policy, that is, what he must do to please his superiors, blends well with the schema the missionary follows to achieve his religious goals. Yet, the *potential* for conflict between these middlemen is present in their pursuit of influence or prestige. It, however, does not occur because the missionary is by far the stronger of the two, his position being so sound that the other cannot challenge it. How then did he achieve this position?

In contrast to the storekeeper, the missionary is actively involved in the daily life of the Naskapi. When he came to Davis Inlet fifteen years ago, all the Naskapi drank constantly, doing little else in the summertime. The missionary saw as his first task bringing an end to the drinking. By actively intervening in the social life of the Naskapi, especially with regard to their drinking behaviour (for example, by breaking up fights), he made many Naskapi turn against him. It is evident that there are definite limits to what a middleman can accomplish with an ethnic group by using such methods. In some way, he must make a platform for himself in the native society; he must find *some* people who are willing to support him.

When the Naskapi started cod fishing five years ago, the missionary imported small outboard engines so that they could buy them for their punts. But they did not have enough cash to do so, whereupon the missionary lent them money on the condition that they stop drinking. Today, almost every household has an outboard engine and five men have bought bigger motorboats, all with help from the missionary. Half the men do, however, still drink.

Besides helping them financially, the missionary renders a variety of other services. There are no hospitals or nurses in Davis Inlet and it is the missionary who gives medical aid, keeping and dispensing a large stock of medicines. He also gives out vitamins and powdered milk to mothers with young children. The missionary says that by winning the mothers through the care of their children, he will in the end "also win the men." Besides being the only man who can give medical help in the community, he is also the only mechanic who can repair and maintain the various machinery in Davis Inlet. In addition, the source of the electric lighting in most of the Naskapi tents is his generator.

The services he renders as a middleman between the Naskapi and the outside world are also of great importance. The missionary operates a radio which he uses to call in the hospital plane in cases of emergency, to send out orders for outboard engines, and so on. With his knowledge of the Naskapi language, he also serves as a necessary link between the Naskapi and the storekeeper, the government officials, and other representatives of Canadian society.

By being a vital communication link between the Naskapi and the outside world, the missionary comes to control a vast amount of information in the community. He also obtains information about the community through the confessions of his parishioners. More important, however, is the fact that the Naskapi come to him with their internecine quarrels and complaints. Consequently, he knows about almost everything that goes on in the community, and he is in a position where he can give support consistently to those who do not drink.

Thus, the missionary as a broker has managed to gain so much influence that, in effect, he becomes the Naskapi patron, a role which he continuously maintains through acts of brokerage. By rendering services and controlling information, he makes himself indispensable to the Naskapi. He has arrived at the position – characteristic of patrons – in which he can make a variety of demands in return for his general stock of prestations. In this position, he is able to put pressure on his "clients" to stop drinking and to behave like good Catholics. The missionary's strategy is made clear by considering the position of those who drink: either they do not have access to some of the goods distributed by the missionary, or they are the last people to enjoy them; this is so, for example, with regard to electric lighting in the tents and outboard motors for the fishing boats.

Yet, one may wonder why the missionary, who desires influence over the Naskapi, encourages them to spend much of their winter on the Barren Grounds where he has no control over them. Indeed, his policy has been to send the children along with their parents for the caribou hunt each autumn. He says that the Naskapi need caribou meat to be healthy, that the parents will not leave without their children, and that the children must learn to survive as hunters in the Barrens.

What the missionary loses in immediate control by leaving the Naskapi alone on the Barrens, however, may be less than what he gains, in the long run. If they lived in Davis Inlet year-round, they would probably learn more English, as well as more about the outside world and the market economy. Most important of all, other middlemen might be attracted, or directed to the community. In these ways, the Naskapi could become less dependent on the missionary.

As is to be expected from the situation outlined above, the missionary is also the cause of conflicts and cleavages among the Naskapi. Today, half the men have stopped drinking. The missionary supports these men whenever he has a chance, and they, in turn, play up to him with the purpose of obtaining something from him. At the same time, the "drinkers" openly oppose the missionary; they gather in small drinking parties where one of the main themes of conversation is how much they dislike him. The non-drinkers seldom enter a tent where there is a drinking party. They must show the missionary that they reject this kind of behaviour and are worthy of his favours, whereas the "drinkers" talk about them and how the missionary supports only the non-drinkers and not themselves. The non-drinkers are caught in a dilemma; they want the support of the missionary, but at the same time they do not want to alienate themselves from those who drink. Whereas those who are opposed to the missionary launch great verbal attacks on him, the non-drinkers never defend him.

In the Barren Grounds, the drinking behaviour does not cause the same kind of cleavage. For example, a man who never takes a drink and has the full support of the missionary shared a tent with a heavy drinker who strongly dislikes, and is disliked by, the missionary. The non-drinker participated in the drinking parties, but never drank himself. Yet, upon returning to Davis Inlet, these two men seldom visited each other. They were divided by the different relationships they had with the missionary.

Two men distinguish themselves as "first men" in the Barren Grounds. They are held in esteem by the Naskapi at the same time as they are opposed to the missionary. Being heavy drinkers when sugar and yeast are available on the coast, it therefore seems reasonable that the missionary wishes to keep them away from Davis Inlet as much as possible. In a bay thirty miles from Davis Inlet, wealthy Americans have been fishing salmon for some years, and each summer they ask the missionary if he could provide two Naskapi as their guides. The missionary offers the job to the two men who accept the offer because it is also in their own interests. They regard themselves as very competent hunters and stress the point that no other Naskapi spend so much of the year in the interior; they want to be identified with the activities of the Barren Grounds as opposed to the economic activities and social life in Davis Inlet. Also, when they stay in Davis Inlet, they are faced with the fact that the missionary exercises greater influence there than they do. Probably, it is important for these two men to impress upon the other Naskapi that they are not clients of the missionary; consequently, they accept his offer and stay away from Davis Inlet.

The missionary did not arrive overnight at his present position of influence in Davis Inlet. An interesting and perhaps crucial feature in the development of his status is his changing relationship with a Naskapi who is popularly known as the "chief" in Davis Inlet. When he arrived in Davis Inlet, he supported from the beginning a Naskapi who had been appointed "chief" in the 1920s by a predecessor – the first missionary to work regularly among these Naskapi. The present missionary built a house for the chief with his own money while the other Naskapi continued to live in tents. He let the chief and one of his sons move into the house on the explicit condition that no beer would be brewed or drunk there; neither the chief nor his son drink today. The missionary plans to make the son chief after his father's death.

There are other ways, too, in which the missionary seeks to support the chief. For example, whenever the missionary leaves the community, he gives the key of the mission house to the chief so that he alone has access to necessary medicines. When guests arrive in the community, the missionary often invites the chief to meet them in his house.

It seems clear that the missionary wishes to impress the authority of the chief and of his son upon the Naskapi and make these two men his principal allies. It may also be that the missionary has set up the chief as a broker between himself and the Naskapi. While this may have been the case before, the chief is *not* in such a position today; in this regard, there has been an interesting change in the strategy of the missionary as *patron*. When he arrived in Davis Inlet, it is probable that he continued to use the chief as a broker as had his predecessor. For one thing, the last shaman of Davis Inlet was still alive and wielding great influence over the Naskapi; he was violently opposed to any missionary and his church. The chief was used, it seems, by the missionary to combat the influence of the shaman. Today, we find that the missionary has direct relations with the Naskapi: he approaches them, and they him, without an intermediary. In fact, it is important for maintaining his position that he distributes personally the resources of his patronage. It is only in a situation where a patron deals directly with his clients that he can be certain that his resources/patronage are enjoyed only by persons willing and able to adopt his values.

However, the chief still has an important role in the missionary's overall strategy. He appears as the *ostensible* spokesman of the Naskapi. This is the explanation, I believe, for the missionary's invitations to the chief to visit his house when officials visit Davis Inlet. For, in this context, it is important that the missionary does not present himself as the patron, or indeed, as the sole spokesman of the Naskapi. Thus, he casts the chief in the role of spokesman while retaining control over the role: speaking to the chief in Naskapi in front of the guests, the missionary tells the chief what should be said to them (in English).

In comparison to the missionary, the storekeeper controls by far the more essential economic and technical resources. It is interesting to consider, then, why the missionary should remain the more influential of the two. The storekeeper, in contrast to the missionary, cannot effectively convert his assets into influence. The storekeeper is *required* to provide the Naskapi with supplies. As a welfare officer, he must distribute goods, without any strings attached, by government order (and the presence of the missionary is a controlling influence). The Naskapi themselves see these as his functions, and they have no feeling of indebtedness to him. Thus, the storekeeper is not in a position to bargain with them.

By contrast, the missionary is required only to preach the Gospel. All other goods and services, he renders to the Naskapi on his own initiative. His goods are not displayed on shelves in a store, but rather are hidden until it is opportune for him to offer them. The usual procedure is to offer something on certain conditions, making it clear that he is doing a particular person a favour and that he can withdraw his services at any time. In this way, he makes the Naskapi dependent upon him in such a way that he can influence their behaviour.

The missionary's position is made easier because of several factors: (1) the Naskapi do not form any corporate groups when they live on the coast; indeed, they are actually divided by their opposite attachments to the missionary; (2) the two most influential men among the Naskapi stay away from the community in the summer; (3) traditional leadership, as understood by the Naskapi, is exemplified by someone taking the initiative in any situation that arises. The chief appointed by the missionary is not such a leader (*wotshimao*); moreover, we have seen that he himself cannot utilize the resources of the missionary or obtain influence through them; (4) it is not easy for the Naskapi to bring about the dismissal of the missionary should they wish to do so (they could, in the case of the storekeeper).

Lastly, the nature of the storekeeper's assets and the restrictions attached to them, combined with his goal of obtaining a promotion and getting out of the community, places him in a position where he needs the missionary as a go-between for himself and the Naskapi. As the storekeeper is unable to control the missionary in his performance of this role, the way is open for the missionary, *qua* go-between for the storekeeper, to act as a broker for himself and his value syndrome. The relationship between these two middlemen, however, remains complementary and uncompetitive. Inasmuch as the storekeeper realizes that the missionary, as his go-between, may "process" information, and thereby practise brokerage, his mind dwells on the available evidence which shows that the missionary is acting on his (the storekeeper's) behalf. It is consistent with the missionary's interests and strategies not to give the storekeeper cause to distrust him.

The storekeeper himself merely wants to be a go-between for the Newfoundland government in its dealings with the Naskapi. The Naskapi try to extract as much as possible from the storekeeper, and he is, ultimately, at their mercy. Should they not like him, they could create trouble and establish an impossible relationship with him so that he would eventually be removed by his superiors. One way the storekeeper might try to prevent this from happening would be to participate in the political life of the Naskapi, competing not only with Naskapi men of influence, but also with the missionary. I have pointed out the difficulties he would have in doing so. He has therefore chosen to avoid any conflicts which might arise in his relations with the Naskapi and the missionary.

The role of the missionary with respect to the storekeeper's need for a go-between is, in fact, replicated *vis-à-vis* the storekeeper's superiors. Whenever these officials come to Davis Inlet, they contact the missionary directly, thus acknowledging that it is he who knows most about the Naskapi. They need the missionary as a translator and as a source of information. As they deal with the missionary alone, the storekeeper's position in the community is weakened in at least two ways. The Naskapi see that they can reach the officials through the missionary without dealing with the storekeeper first. Further, the missionary is in a position where he can report on the activities of the storekeeper directly to his superiors. Thus, the missionary has extensive control over the community. Besides being a patron of the Naskapi independent of the government, he is also an indispensable person for the government in its dealings with the Naskapi.

It only remains to be added that the position of the missionary in Davis Inlet is that much stronger because *he* does not need a go-between between himself and his clients.

The Meaningfulness of the Two Worlds of the Naskapi

7

Living among the Naskapi in Davis Inlet, one quickly learns that they are much less enthusiastic about fishing cod than hunting caribou. While sitting in their punts in a bay jigging cod, they often say, "Fishing is no good – too hard work. Only hunting any good. Hunting is not work." For an outsider, these remarks may seem strange when one compares the relatively easy job of fishing cod with the harsh and strenuous life of a hunter. Obviously, the Naskapi are not basing their assessment on the time or the physical effort put into these two activities, but rather on other values. A further clue to the fact that the hunting of caribou is especially meaningful is provided by the following incident.

A group of men were lying on the beach, biding time before hauling their traps again. From across the bay on a mountain side, they spotted some black rocks in a patch of snow. Suddenly, one man started talking about the rocks as if they were caribou. The other men joined in, and an excited discussion followed about how many caribou there were, whether they were moving or lying still, and so on. Some men ran off for their binoculars. When asked whether they were really caribou, the men laughed and answered "of course it is only rocks," and continued their noisy debate about the sham caribou. The next morning, some of the men went hunting, remaining as long as a week in the middle of the short cod season.

There are many similar indications that the Naskapi find the world of the interior more gratifying and meaningful than the coastal world. Yet, the Naskapi move down to Davis Inlet in the spring because they find something of value there also. They appreciate the company of all the people they are separated from during the winter. They also value the safety and comfort of the village where store goods and medicines can be obtained at any time. They are attracted to the white world and what it has to offer in the way of material goods. They are also, of course, dependent upon the trade in Davis Inlet to continue their life in the Barren Grounds. Nevertheless, the fact that the Naskapi repeatedly say, while on the coast, that they only look forward to the day they can return to the interior, indicates that they believe they can pursue something of great value there which they cannot do on the coast.

What, then, is implied in the term "meaningfulness"? I shall not attempt a rigorous and operational definition of the term. Rather, I hope that the reader will sense the validity of the notion as I proceed with the discussion of the two worlds of the Naskapi.

I have already argued that the Naskapi culture, as it unfolds in the interior world, shows an integration of its various elements and a relative consistency of values. I have also explained why the important cultural complex of hunting, sharing, prestige, and leadership does not function on the coast. In this chapter, I shall explain why the Naskapi culture on the coast is marked by disintegration of its various elements and an inconsistency of values. It is in the context of these cultural characteristics and their implications that I speak of the relative meaningfulness of the two worlds of the Naskapi.

We have seen that there are two fundamental dilemmas in the Naskapi culture which are also present in the Barren Ground world: sharing versus having, and autonomy versus safety (by being a follower of a good hunter). This opposition we may call *internal inconsistency* of values insofar as the maximization of one value negates the maximization of another. This inconsistency represents itself to the actor as a dilemma. In spite of this, I shall maintain that the interior world is generally marked by an internal *consistency* of values as the opportunity situation induces the actor to pursue a set of values, none of which seriously jeopardizes the maximization of the other values in the complex. For example, by hunting caribou and sharing the meat, the hunter stands to gain values such as role confirmation, prestige, and leadership. At the same time, there are few opportunities to do otherwise in the interior, such as keeping the meat for oneself and later converting it into cash. In addition, as we shall see, the Naskapi have their own sanctions against deviating from accepted behaviour.

Thus, the Naskapi culture in the interior world is integrated, in the sense that all members share a set of central values which are realized in action in a Naskapi environment; that is, the Barren Ground world, as an opportunity situation is consistent with these values. This means that under similar conditions, almost every Naskapi will make similar choices and act in a similar fashion to maximize the shared values. These choices and actions constitute what is called institutionalized behaviour.

That choices and actions are institutionalized implies, then, that the Naskapi share the values involved in them. Furthermore, it means that they agree upon the contexts in which the various shared values are relevant, and how different values relate to each other within the same context. While this is, to a large extent, the case in the interior, we shall see that the Naskapi have difficulties in agreeing about them on the coast. This has several effects on the social life of the two worlds; the two which I shall be concerned with here are conflict and ritual.

In discussing ritual, I shall take Leach (1954) as my starting point. From his point of view, "technique and ritual, profane and sacred, do not denote *types* of action but *aspects* of almost any kind of action. Technique has economic material consequences which are measurable and predictable; ritual on the other hand is a symbolic statement which 'says' something about the individuals involved in the action" (pp. 12–13). However, as Barth (1964) has pointed out: "We need to be able to distinguish between rituals as systems of communication, and the mere fact that all actions, no matter how pragmatic, have 'meanings' to the persons who observe them. Though Durkheim's dichotomy of sacred and profane is untenable, the feeling remains that rituals are actions especially pregnant with meaning, that they are at least in a relative sense set apart from other acts, for one thing because they are, in a sense more important. Very tentatively, then, one might say that *ritual is the symbolic aspect of acts in contexts vested with particular value*" (p. 147) (my emphasis). Barth also points out that "there is no reason why the very forms of an act which reflect the technical imperatives may not *also* be vested with central and crucial meaning in a symbolic system or context" (*loc. cit.*).

Taking Barth's definition of ritual, we are still left with the difficult task of sorting out those contexts which are vested with particular values from those contexts which have less value. If we say that ritual is a corporate activity in which a group of people jointly communicate about shared values, it seems reasonable to argue that some shared values lend themselves more easily and frequently to ritual communication than others. In addition to a difference in the degree of communication, there would also seem to be some difference in the quality of the ritual. Thus, among the Naskapi where equality is a value, the maximization of values that lead to inequality must be undercommunicated. Such aspects of actions are called negative ritual (Durkheim, 1965:338; Goffman, 1967:73). While negative rituals indicate a distance between the actors that must be concealed, or a dilemma that must be coped with, positive rituals express the shared values around which the group is corporated. It is in this positive sense that I discuss ritual; since ritual says something first and foremost about the individuals involved in the action and about the action itself, we can say that ritual communication is primarily about corporate action which, in itself, is a shared value.

My assertion is that we can speak of Naskapi society as a corporate group if we make the assumption that a basic human need is to be accepted as a social person by other people. The individual manages this by acting out certain role behaviour in front of people who are willing to accept his behaviour and verify the image the individual has of himself. Furthermore, the role behaviour that is most important to the individual is usually played out in groups where the individual is more or less guaranteed recognition and verification of his image and values. Thus, if the individual feels that his role play is unsuccessful outside, he can retreat to one of "his" groups and there seek the recognition he did not get outside. In this connection, the function of friendship is relevant in that an individual can seek a friend's confidence regarding his worries about his relations with the group; also, "a person is able to see himself in his friend" (Paine, 1969:507). In a society where an individual can belong to many groups, a person can oscillate between them, seeking support from one group when another fails. He may also have the option of seeking a new group whose value system is more congenial to him and in which he can change his role behaviour correspondingly.

Such reference groups have a system of shared values against which certain aspects of the members' behaviour are evaluated. I call such values corporate values since the members of the group all contribute to the management and maintenance of these values, and since the members all benefit from them and maximize them through cooperation.

Furthermore, in a reference group, the contexts in which the group's corporate values are circulating are the ones most vested with meaning and in which ritual behaviour will be most intense.

I am suggesting, then, that we can view the Naskapi as corporated around a set of shared values to which they are all committed, and with reference to which they evaluate each other and upon which they are thus dependent to gain the social recognition each individual seeks. These corporate values are all the more central and important as all adult males are incumbents of the same statuses, with everybody sharing the most important status – that of being a hunter. Thus, every Naskapi male is evaluated according to how good a hunter he is, how good a provider he is, and how good a husband and father he is. As was shown in chapters 2 and 3, a man attains recognition and prestige from his fellows by being skilled in subsistence activities, and accordingly, all Naskapi men must exhibit largely the same role behaviour. Since there are no groups in their society in which an individual can seek alternative recognition as a substitute for the acknowledgement he can get as a hunter, the Naskapi society as a whole can be seen as one reference group with a pool of corporate values which all the members must manage and maintain. Those contexts where these values are played out are those most vested with meaning.

Let us turn to the system of values with reference to which the Naskapi explicitly evaluate each other's behaviour, and investigate how these values are communicated in different contexts. In chapters 2 and 3, we saw that the Naskapi have means by which every individual can display his expertise and ability as a hunter and obtain rewards in the forms of prestige and role reinforcement. By going out hunting when most of the men prefer to stay in camp, or by returning home later than the others, one gets recognition for one's deeds from the whole camp which waits tensely for one's return to hear an account of the day's hunt.[1] We have also seen that anybody can set

---

1. I used this technique to obtain recognition and verification that I was a man and a hunter, the hunter status being the only one I could fill and get rewards from. Having no chance to act out the roles relevant to my own culture in the Barren Grounds, I experienced the need for recognition from the people around me; in other words, I had to adopt and incorporate Naskapi values to stay alive as a sane and social person.

out as a *wotshimao* and thus be given recognition. Hence, central values are shared, ritually re-affirmed (through *mokoshan)* and used in awarding prestige to any member of the society who exhibits proper behaviour.

The following series of events is typical and illustrative of the above comments. In a small camp of three tents, Luke was *wotshimao.* One day, three men among whom Fred was *wotshimao,* arrived from Davis Inlet in just two days. Luke, as host, bedded and feasted these men (thereby gaining prestige and an audience for his stories). The next day Fred went hunting alone and killed nine caribou. Upon his return to the camp, it was his turn to be the storyteller and be the object of praise. In the evening, *mokoshan* was held and Fred distributed the *pmin.* The following morning, Fred left with his companions wearing the mocassins Luke had given him to replace his own worn ones.

The preceding account illustrates how different values are brought into play and communicated. Sharing and hospitality are stressed by Luke in his reception of the three men. His visitors, on the other hand, recognize Luke's right to communicate the importance of his roles as *wotshimao,* as the first man to travel into the Barrens, and as a skilful hunter, by being his attentive and encouraging audience. The next day, it was Fred's turn to receive acknowledgement for his success in hunting.

Although all the men in camp were present in the audience in Luke's tent, there was a difference in the degree to which they took part in the prestige-giving. Luke, the great hunter in his prime, could afford to be lavish in his praise of Fred; but one man in his fifties who had had a reputation as a good hunter and who was now surpassed by younger men, participated with less enthusiasm and spent less time in Luke's tent than the others. He also once indicated that he hoped to be *wotshimao* in another camp; when another man became *wotshimao,* he spent considerably less time in the ensuing rituals of *mokoshan.*

There is no doubt that it is difficult for the older hunters to afford younger men prestige. Yet they do, and they continue to participate in the competition for prestige and leadership as long as they are able to.

The account above also shows that the two chief contenders for prestige were the ones who most actively gave it. It was first Fred, and the next day Luke who most vigorously praised the other. Conflict was avoided here because anyone seeking recognition from the others does so only in connection with specific actions; it is after having completed an act that a hunter will play up to an audience. As in the case of Luke and Fred, the competitors usually seek separate occasions (audiences) for the giving and receiving of prestige.

However, one must still account for the fact that competitors themselves give each other recognition and prestige. It must be stressed again that every adult male seeks and obtains social recognition for the same kind of actions, and thus they are in a sense competitors. Yet, at the same time as they are acting with reference to the same values and contending for the same rewards, they are also *dependent on each other* for the very same values and rewards. Only through a communal effort are they able to maintain the value system with which they reward one another. Hence, a hunter cannot refuse recognition of the other man without denying the validity of the standards by which the hunter himself wishes to be judged.

By the same token, the best hunters may also be the most zealous in giving each other esteem: the more enthusiasm Fred could muster in praising Luke, the more he could expect from Luke the next day. There were no difficulties entailed in this exchange as Fred was staying in the same camp as Luke was only a few days. But this is not always the case. We saw above that the aging hunter withdrew from ritual prestige-giving because he felt that he did not receive the recognition he deserved. We also noted that one of the main reasons why the Naskapi split into smaller camps is the desire of the hunters to be *wotshimao* and to gain prestige where there will be less competition.

It has been shown that the Naskapi share the values of autonomy and prestige. Each individual tries to maximize his autonomy at the same time as he recognizes the value of "followership" and safety, but also competes for prestige and a following. This inconsistency in values is an inherent dilemma in the culture and is potentially disruptive of social life. To maximize the autonomy value, one must either withdraw from any interaction that implies the loss of autonomy, or seek influence over other people and thereby maintain one's own autonomy.

Both these strategies are common and both of them are potentially disruptive to the society. The first tends to split the society into minimum-sized autonomous groups (households), while the second implies encroachment on the autonomy of one's followers and has the same result. Thus, the only way out of this dilemma is either to disperse into the smallest possible units, or retreat to an environment where people can be safe without being followers. We have seen that the latter option obtains on the coast where the Naskapi can do without followership. However, the security they need is gained only by becoming clients of the white man, the result of which is a loss of autonomy for the individual Naskapi as well as for his society.

In the Barren Grounds, however, the Naskapi do follow good hunters as leaders. How, then, are they able to handle the dilemma inherent in the leader–follower relationship? In chapter 3, I suggested that they cope with this conflict by the leaders exercising a very limited and indirect influence, and by communicating equality.

It is clear why this must be so since the Naskapi communicate about the values and ideas they have about the proper role behaviour of a man and a hunter through their very competitive behaviour. Travelling at a fast pace is one way of communicating these values. By this act, one not only reaffirms the fact that each individual shares them, but one's role behaviour is recognized and approved of, also. Since both the good and the poor hunters, the fast and the slow travellers are equally dependent upon this communication and recognition, the leaders must keep within the boundaries of proper behaviour. If a *wotshimao* exerted too much leadership, his followers would leave him. Thus, it is partly through ritual communication of corporate values with a concomitant undercommunication of inequality and influence that the Naskapi are able to cope with this value inconsistency.

Finally, another point should be mentioned with regard to situations where the tendency to a hierarchical structure in Naskapi society is made more or less explicit. Different situations can be interpreted diversely by the various participants. Hence, the chief of *mokoshan* can interpret the ritual as one which, above all, confirms his position as one of the best hunters. At the same time, the other hunters may interpret the ritual as one where the equality and interdependence of all men are stressed and communicated. This dual interpretation should not jeopardize, in any way, the function of the ritual in reaffirming the shared and corporate values involved.

The same dual interpretation can be made by the men who are travelling together. The *wotshimao* prefers to believe that he is pulling the others with him in the race, while his followers think they can travel just as fast and that they are all equal. They have, of course, good reasons to interpret the situation in this way. Often a group finds that the *wotshimao* is travelling too slowly and therefore leave him behind. Also, sometimes a *wotshimao* wants to set up camp too early, and his followers have to encourage him to travel on.

Besides these shared values around which the Naskapi are corporated, they have a much wider system of meanings through which they communicate non-verbally and which is ritual in the sense that it takes place in contexts vested with extreme value. For example, when a group of families is travelling and living together in the Barren Grounds, they are certainly communicating unity and interdependence just by living in that environment which they perceive as potentially dangerous and towards which they have ambivalent feelings. Hence, when they set up camp in bad weather, they put up their tents close together to feel secure in an environment which can be friendly or hostile. Indeed, their whole culture is geared towards mastery of this environment and its animal species. Their mythology emphasizes the close relationship between man and his natural surroundings, a relationship which is also reflected in their social organization. Through the institution of common sharing, they are saying that they must live or perish as a group. Moreover, as we have already seen, the Naskapi evaluate much of their actions with direct reference to the physical environment. It is prestigious to travel long distances in a short time, and to defy storms, hunger, and other trials which nature may bring forth.

This total context and their position in it are probably the themes over which they communicate when a whole camp engages in playful hunts after squirrels and otters. Similarly, through the great excitement and joy that breaks out when new people are discovered approaching a camp, the Naskapi find expression for and communicate their isolation in the wilderness, their unity as a group, and also their bonds with other Naskapi scattered over the Barren Grounds.

Moreover, the intense decision-making process in which everybody engages during the incessant visiting between tents, and the tense wait for a *wotshimao* to leave the camp, must have ritual aspects in order that everybody agrees about what is involved in this kind of situation and that it be important and worth pursuing.

In the Barren Grounds, most, if not all, activities take place in contexts that are vested with tremendous value and meaning for the Naskapi. They reflect their links with the natural, mythological, and social realms of the Naskapi culture. Thus, through the activities involved in hunting and sharing meat, the hunter is simultaneously interacting with the physical environment, the animal spirits, and his fellow Naskapi. He cannot separate them, since they are interrelated. If a Naskapi does not adhere to the proper code of behaviour, he is sanctioned not only by his society but also by the animal spirits that control the physical environment and his luck in hunting.

I have argued that the integrated culture of the Naskapi in the Barren Ground world enables them to define situations or contexts in terms of the values and meanings that are involved; further, that there are many contexts that are rendered more meaningful in that shared and corporate values are circulated and are communicated non-verbally through ritual aspects of actions.

In contrast to the interior world, the activities in the coastal world are relatively devoid of such ritual communication. I am not able to measure the difference in operational terms, but it seems reasonable that my assessment is correct since non-verbal symbolic communication must be based on shared values and meanings and must take place in defined contexts in which the actors agree upon the values circulated. I maintain that the main reason for the lack of ritual on the coast is caused by a failure to institutionalize behaviour with regard to crucial values; that is, they are unable to define unambiguously the situations or contexts in which particular values are agreed to be important and how they should circulate in relation to each other. This is part of the disintegration of the Naskapi culture on the coast: crucial and shared values no longer exhibit internal consistency. The numerous conflicts that characterize life on the coast testify to this fact.

The most frequent conflicts arise from economic transactions in Davis Inlet where the traditional ideas about such transactions clash with the choices made on the basis of the new opportunities provided by a money economy. Not only have new articles from the outside with their associated cash value started to circulate, but also goods and services which traditionally were shared, exchanged in kind, or rendered free, have gained a cash value. As was mentioned previously, the tradition of sharing is quickly breaking down in Davis Inlet, itself. The Naskapi are aware of these discordant ideas of evaluation; they talk about the inconsistency of the "new ideas" with the old ones, or with that which is "real" Indian.

Thus, the individual Naskapi is caught in a dilemma: should he give something away without asking for anything in return, or should he ask to be paid in kind or in cash? Should he give it away, or should he keep it for his own consumption, or for later sale to the store or other white men? He is caught in the same dilemma when asked to lend his equipment. If he does lend it, should he ask for money or not? The Naskapi have not managed to solve these problems, an indication of their inability to institutionalize transactions involving cash among themselves. Thus, the traditional rules of sharing and redistribution (ritually sanctioned or not) are still influential, if sometimes only covertly, in nearly every transaction involving any kind of goods. Although two parties may agree upon a price in cash, the transaction may later be the cause of an open conflict because the buyer feels that he should have been given the commodity free, or for a much lower price. A man once gave away a new trout net. Several years later, he still reviles, when drunk, the receiver for not paying him for it. The man who took the net, however, claims that it was given to him free.

Because the Naskapi have difficulty in defining what is involved in their transactions, and because of the resultant failure of institutionalization, the price is arbitrarily set in each new transaction. In addition, it is usually set far too high in relation to the market value of the commodity involved. For example, a man paid thirty dollars for renting a canoe for only two days. Later, he resented the owner for taking so much money.

In some cases, high prices are due to earlier unsettled transactions. In others, factors of kinship and leadership may be involved. One case involved two men (A and B) who are married to sisters and A is also the maternal uncle of B. A is an extremely able hunter, while B is a rather poor one. B usually follows A into the interior when they go hunting, often living in A's tent, and he receives from A what meat and skins his family needs. One winter when B stayed on the coast, A rented two of B's dogs for two months, paying sixty dollars for them. In addition, he gave B one of his own dogs when he returned to Davis Inlet. This is an excess amount when compared with the purchase price of one full-grown dog which is six dollars. Although A later indicated that he had paid too much money, he had certainly confirmed his generosity and superiority.

The dilemma between traditional sharing and cash transactions is illustrated in the ambivalent attitude towards the disposal of caribou skin products. Although the Naskapi have this problem in the interior also, they sell skins or skin products only to each other on the coast.

In the interior, I once suggested to the oldest active hunter (who was about 58 years old) that he make a lot of moccasins from his caribou skins in order to sell them. Basing my calculation on what he shot last year, I told him that he could have made close to one thousand dollars. In response to this suggestion, he worked himself into a terrific rage, saying that he could never sell moccasins. "If some people are hungry, I must give them food. A man without moccasins can't go hunting. He and his family will be hungry, down, dead and cold. I must give him moccasins if I have any. No Sir, I cannot sell moccasins." The next day he told me that it was alright to sell skin products to white people, but never to the Indians. However, this man, like everybody else, *does* sell hides and other skin products to other Naskapi on the coast.

It must be a constant reminder of this dilemma, and a temptation to break the traditional rules of sharing when a man sees the recipients of his skins later sell them for cash. Even if only a small fraction of what he gives away is sold, he is still aware that his skins represent a lot of money. A good hunter may well shoot 100 caribou in a winter. Reckoning that he will get 4 pairs of moccasins each worth $4.50, from one skin, his skins represent a value of $1,800. As it is, he has to give away nearly all his skins to those who shoot very few or no caribou at all. For the good hunter, this means little cash but for the community as a whole, it means that everybody receives enough skins for moccasins and snowshoes.

Similarly, one man shot a beaver which he, according to the rules, gave to another man accompanying him on the hunt. He told me that "by and by, that man will get plenty of money for the pelt."

In spite of this knowledge of opportunity costs, I can cite only one case from the interior in which somebody attempted to override the rules of sharing. Because the case illustrates both the significance of rituals among the Naskapi and how they can be the basis of social sanctions, I shall relate the incident in some detail.

Three families left a large camp to establish a new camp further into the interior. Soon after, the two most capable hunters shot forty caribou. A few days later, they were joined by another six families, among whom was the *wotshimao osken* for the *mokoshan* to be held later. The newcomers said they had no meat left, and that their dogs were hungry. Normally they would at once have been given meat and skins without asking for it. But this time, they received nothing. All the newcomers assembled in one tent, discussed the matter, and agreed that this was not proper behaviour, and that the three men were not good Indians. They also recalled that one of the three men originally came to Davis Inlet from another band. "Those people (from that band) are always stingy, and they don't look after *mokoshan* properly, treating the *pmin* carelessly." Everybody was upset. One man even left with his family a few days later, saying that "somebody has plenty of food while I am hungry."

Doubtless, the three men refrained from distributing their meat because they wanted to keep the skins for themselves. They said they were returning to Davis Inlet soon, implying that they had no more time to get hold of as many skins as they desired. Also, the wives of the hunters who shot the caribou are the most industrious women in Davis Inlet when it comes to making moccasins for sale to the store.

Finally, the time came to have *mokoshan* in the camp. The ritual was announced three days in advance. However, the evening before the prescribed day, the *wotshimao osken* (one of the newcomers) announced that he could not participate because he had to make a scaffold that day. The result was that no ritual was held. Indeed, it would have been impossible to perform the ceremony since it affirms the values of common sharing and interdependence. (As it turned out, the *wotshimao osken* did not build a scaffold.)

After this incident, the three men distributed their meat and skins, and *mokoshan* was performed shortly after. Thus, the sanctions operating in the Barren Ground world are so strong that it is difficult for an individual to break the rules in order to maximize the opportunities for earning cash.

Conflicts over economic matters are frequent even among the closest relatives. For example, a man came into my tent and said that he was fed up with all the gossip and quarrels in Davis Inlet, and that he was now quarrelling with his own brothers. He had borrowed a rifle from one of his brothers and his brother did not like that. On the other hand, he had given one porcupine and four ptarmigan to his brother without receiving any money, but "I don't care about that," he added. He then said that he would not stay and work in Davis Inlet during the summer "because there is too much gossip and quarrel in the community."

In another case I was drawn in as a mediator between a married daughter and her parents when she accused them of stealing one of her monthly family allowance cheques.

The free lending of equipment which is bought with savings or borrowed money also entails difficulties. This is easy to understand when one considers the carelessness with which the Naskapi handle all material goods.

For instance, a man once borrowed a seal net and did not bother to take it up when the ice settled in the autumn.

It is symptomatic that the greatest frequency of conflicts are of an economic kind arising from the dilemma of sharing versus having. Fulfilling the obligation of sharing is problematic, while not sharing causes resentment. One man who is an avid seal hunter, complained to the missionary about the fact that he had to give away all his seals to the young men who accompanied him in his boat. He said there was no use in his pursuing the seal hunt as he made no profit out of it. On the other hand, a man who took the other alternative and refused to give or even share the seal he shot with his companion caused bitter feelings.

In an earlier chapter, we saw why the Naskapi in the coastal world do not gain prestige and leadership by sharing produce; at the same time, they have the opportunity to maximize their individual economic careers by saving, and buying luxury goods and capital equipment such as fishing boats and motor toboggans. It has become profitable to keep, save, and sell.

On the coast, this dilemma of sharing versus having militates against communication over corporate values since the actors disagree about the values involved in any specific context. They share, to a great extent, the values that are involved, but disagree on how they should circulate within any one context. Hence, while one party in a situation finds it profitable to sell or keep his goods, the other party will find it profitable to claim that the goods be shared. It is obvious that little if any ritual activity would take place under such circumstances.

In the Barren Ground world, it was shown that the ideal of sharing is crucial to the maintenance of corporate values and that sharing lends value and meaning to hunting and other subsistence activities. On the coast, because people disagree about the applicability of the rules of sharing, there is no consensus as to what constitutes the proper role behaviour of a hunter in the coastal world. The successful seal hunter would like to keep the seal for himself, yet knowing that other people would resent this. He also knows that other people keep their produce when they get something, but as an audience that should give him recognition for his skills and role behaviour, they still want him to share. It is therefore very difficult for the Naskapi to appreciate any on-going activity since the activity itself is pregnant with conflict rather than value and ritual meaning.

In the Barren Ground world, it is the *activity* which is of the greatest value and which conveys meaning through its ritual aspect. Of course, meat itself is valuable as food, but it is given additional value by the place it has in the social and ritual life. The subsistence activities in the Barren Ground world are joint activities insofar as everybody is acting with reference to corporate values. Hence, while the Naskapi may strive for material goods, safety, and comfort in the interior, also, they must do so in groups where the activities themselves are of primary value.

In the coastal world, however, values such as material goods, safety, and comfort can be obtained just as well, or better, through individual efforts whereby the economic activities are deprived of corporate values. Here, material goods and comfort become the *objects* of the personal gain while the activities themselves are secondary and void of social value. Moreover, whenever an individual keeps, saves, or sells anything that could have been shared, other Naskapi actually stand to lose (when the rules of common sharing could have been applied). On these grounds, it is difficult for the Naskapi to establish a system of corporate values and meanings over which they can communicate through rituals.

In conclusion, then, since the economic activities on the coast have such little social and ritual meaning for the Naskapi, so the coastal world itself has little cultural meaning for them.

Postscript: The Future of the Naskapi

> ... "man (must) become aware of mankind. It is on the
> level of human awareness that virtually all solutions to
> the great problems must now lie."
>
> C. W. Mills

Having lived and participated in the daily life of a small society such as the Naskapi for one and a half years, on parting, one feels that one is leaving something of oneself behind. Indeed, perhaps one never loses the feeling that an essential part of oneself belongs with the people whom one has left. The more one has internalized some of the fundamental values of the society, and felt a need to act according to them in order to be recognized as a social person and a member of the group, the more likely it is that one has found a new meaning and sense of purpose for one's own life within that culture and on that culture's own premises. The climax of the anthropologist's experience must be when he comes to realize that his whole life gains new dimensions through participation in a culture so different from his own. When this happens, the anthropologist has not only theoretically, but personally, discovered and experienced a way of life that is an alternative to his own. He has become aware of some aspects of his own personality and some dimensions in human and social life that were unknown to him before.

He is then in a situation in which he cannot avoid comparing his own culture and society, and his own life within it, with that strange way of life that is no longer strange but intensely meaningful to him. This comparison implies, of necessity, an evaluation of the different world views and life styles of diverse cultures. In doing so, the anthropologist is bound to reach the conclusion that his way of life in his own culture is not the only one possible, nor perhaps the most desirable.

This book is about a culture and society fundamentally different from the Euro-Canadian, yet contained within the borders of Canada. All Canadians are aware of the existence of Indians within their country, and that they have a different cultural background than their own. However, the view commonly held is that the Indians (and Eskimos) by now have lost the greater part of their cultural heritage, and that today, they are merely eking out a living on the fringe of the Euro-Canadian society. The opinion of most politicians and the general public is that these peoples must be assimilated as soon as possible so that their standard of living can improve in proportion to the economic growth of Canada, and so that they can make their contribution to it.

This opinion is based on two major assumptions which are widely held among the peoples of the western civilization. The first is that a high standard of living is universally desirable; it is materially defined and measured according to a scale of material acquisitions and well-being. The second assumption is that western cultures and societies are superior in most, if not all respects, to the cultures and societies of the Eskimos and Indians. Indeed, most of us seem to think that we are superior to all other cultures on earth, and that total assimilation, or at least an adoption of our ways, is inevitable. Hence, western man feels that he is doing these other societies a favour by bringing in his bulldozers and by teaching them the ways of the West. This is not necessarily so.

The crucial point and the fatal error is that the excellence of western societies as well as the rest of the world, is measured almost solely in terms of economics (and power politics). Societies and cultures everywhere have come into contact with the industrialized nations, and in this confrontation, they are fighting a losing battle for their social and cultural integrity. In my view, a most important problem is how to protect these cultures from disintegration and at the same time help them to attain an effective bargaining position *vis-à-vis* the outside world wherein they can choose what they want, and reject what they do not want from the industrialized world.

Recognizing the intrinsic value of every culture as a different expression of mankind, we should respect all peoples and cultures. Indeed, because we are economically and technologically the stronger, it seems to me that it is our *duty* to help other cultures *resist* the intrusion of our culture to the extent that they wish. Instead, we are doing our best to destroy and assimilate them.

Turning to Davis Inlet, for many years the provincial government and the medical and school personnel in North West River and Happy Valley have been pressuring the Naskapi to move to the Indian community in North West River.[1] The rationale for such a move has been, and is, that it would be easier and cheaper to provide the Naskapi with education and medical attention there. It would also speed up the process of assimilation.

The arguments against such a move are many. First of all, while it may be easier to provide the Naskapi with needed services, it would probably

---

1. In 1958, all the Naskapi were promised jobs if they moved to North West River. Seventeen families left Davis Inlet, but found that there was no work for them and no fresh meat to eat. Eleven families returned to Davis Inlet. Three of the six families that remained either had or contracted T.B. Later, the Naskapi had from time to time unanimously voted to stay in Davis Inlet. The last time was in 1966 before they started clearing the ground for the new village.

not be any cheaper. At least today, a move to North West River would mean that almost all the Naskapi would go on welfare the whole year-round, while in Davis Inlet, they could probably manage without any relief if they were given a little more assistance in the utilization of the resources in the Davis Inlet area. Moving to North West River would also mean a deterioration of their diet, as they would have to rely on the inferior food available in the store. This would lead to poorer health and a higher frequency of hospitalization. Today, the Naskapi generally enjoy good health because of their fresh meat diet (in contrast to the Montagnais in North West River).

Finally, and by far the most important, is that the Naskapi culture is a hunting culture; to move them south where there are no opportunities for hunting would imply the end of the Naskapi as an Indian people with their dignity and cultural identity intact. A sudden change to another environment and to other kinds of employment would surely result in a loss of culture and integrity; they would simply become an underprivileged proletariat living in shanties on the outskirts of the white society. Even if they acquired a television set, they would have left behind what, in a *real* sense, gave them their high "standard of living" in their northern wilderness – their culture and way of life. The Naskapi in Davis Inlet have a chance to avoid this tragic fate.

Of course, Naskapi culture is not static. Being compelled to adapt to the outside world, Naskapi culture and society are changing rapidly. Evidence of such changes and the extent to which this is a painful process for them have been given in the latter part of this book. In this, we can do little to relieve them. They must, amongst themselves, battle out new codes of behaviour. But we can help by providing them with economic and technical assistance to utilize the local resources, and by furnishing them with as much information as they require to be able to make rational choices.

As it is today, the Naskapi are making choices that may have unwanted consequences which they do not foresee; for example, moving into insulated houses, and adopting motor toboggans. The Naskapi see the advantages of leaving their families behind in houses during the winter for the sake of the comfort and safety found in Davis Inlet. The children could then attend school regularly, the store would provide the necessary food, and the missionary the medicines and emergency treatment. For the men, it would mean less cumbersome trips into the interior.

The Naskapi have started to buy motor toboggans with which they can travel swiftly into the Barrens in the winter and come back to their families with fresh caribou meat. This pattern of exploitation is likely to have profound effects on the hunting economy of the Naskapi. First, the social setting in the interior will be different with no women and children present in the short-lived hunting camps (they would stay behind in Davis Inlet). Secondly, because this modern equipment is expensive to use, the Naskapi will be in even greater need of cash than before, and therefore will have to centre their economic production on the coast rather than on the interior. They will be compelled to alter their yearly round of activities and to exploit their environment in a similar fashion to the settler. Thirdly, the emphasis on cash is likely to force a re-evaluation of the caribou and its products. The owner of a motor toboggan is well aware of the costs of maintenance and gasoline.

Furthermore, the amount of meat that a toboggan can hold is considerably less than a sled's capacity, pulled by dogs. As a result, a hunter is more bound to compare the costs of procuring caribou with what he gets in return by giving it away to others. The dilemma of evaluating what is involved in their transactions will probably reach a point where the solution, in my opinion, will have to be the giving way of the traditional rules of sharing in favour of cash transactions. But this process will take a long time and give rise to many conflicts among the Naskapi.

Such a complicated series of social and cultural "events" are perhaps uncontrollable, no matter how much information the actors themselves possess. Nevertheless, the ideal should be that every individual in the society be able both to grasp and influence the historical process in which he has a part (Mills, 1959). Given the small scale of the Naskapi society, it should be possible, theoretically, to come close to this ideal. But this necessitates that the Naskapi gain a bird's eye view both of their own culture and society and of the outside world and their relation to it. At least, they could then avoid a move similar to the one they made in 1958 (see footnote 1).

What I am suggesting, then, is that the Naskapi would be better off in all respects if they chose and were allowed to remain in Davis Inlet. This is contingent on their being given a fair chance to establish a bargaining position *vis-à-vis* the outside world. In this they need help of various kinds such as economic and technological aid, adequate information about the outside world and their relations with it, and a more adequate educational system directed towards their own situation. Today, the Naskapi struggle through the first grades in school until they are fifteen or sixteen years old, trying to learn what is supposed to be good for white city dwellers. White middle-class values are forced upon the young Naskapi through an education that is largely irrelevant to their social and cultural background, and to the natural environment which they must later exploit to make a living.

I wish to make a final point. The views above are often brushed aside as being romantic. It follows from the development of my argument that this judgement is clearly unjustified. Be that as it may, one may also argue in terms of global ecology. Taking all the evidence available today, one is justified in arriving at the conclusion that the modern industrial states are overdeveloped, and that in future, we will have to de-escalate our rate of production and consumption (cf. Schumacher, 1970). Accordingly, different kinds of intermediate adaptations may be a necessity in the future. Thus, such an adaptation as the Naskapi are struggling to make in northern Labrador is just as valuable, and certainly more sound ecologically, than our own adaptation to the total environment.

Afterword

Georg Henriksen (1940–2007) first lived among the Mushuau Innu[1] of northern Labrador in the late 1960s at a pivotal point in their history as they made the difficult transition from a form of social organization based on nomadic caribou hunting to a highly sedentary one based in a coastal, government-built village where they rapidly became dependent on government transfer payments. *Hunters in the Barrens* bears witness to the end of the Innu's nomadic way of life, while at the same time pointing to the precursors of various social pathologies which in later years would attract international attention.

In 1975, at the invitation of the Native Association of Newfoundland and Labrador (NANL), Georg returned to Davis Inlet (Utshimassit) to conduct research for an Innu "statement of claim" under the Canadian government's comprehensive land claims policy which was established in 1973 as a modern-day treaty-making process for non-treaty Aboriginal peoples throughout Canada. Along with their Innu neighbours in Sheshatshiu to the south, the Mushuau Innu broke away from NANL in 1976 to form the Naskapi Montagnais Innu Association, and submitted their claim to the federal government the following year.[2] Georg's scholarly and political engagement with the Innu continued thereafter.

I first met Georg in 1983 at an "advocacy and anthropology" conference at Memorial University. I had read *Hunters in the Barrens* by that point in the context of graduate studies at the university and had greatly appreciated its sensitive, analytical perspective. I could see that Georg's 1960s fieldwork was the beginning of a lifelong concern for the well-being of the Innu, and one that informed his involvement with the International Work Group for Indigenous Affairs which he co-founded in 1968, as well as the paper he gave at the Memorial conference. The paper cautioned advocacy anthropologists

---

1. Nowadays, the Innu throughout Labrador and Quebec refer to themselves as Innu (singular) or Innuat (plural). The Labrador Innu with whom Georg worked, and who were formerly referred to as Naskapi, refer to themselves nowadays as Mushuau Innu (or Mushuaunnuat in standard orthography).

2. The name of the organization was changed to the Innu Nation in 1990. Formal land claim negotiations between the Innu and the governments of Newfoundland and Canada began in 1991.

about the dangers of entering into patron–client relationships with Aboriginal people and furthering "the colonial processes still at work by stealing crucial decisions and political initiatives" from them.[3]

Georg heeded this caution throughout his professional life, but remained preoccupied with the perplexing issue stated succinctly in the postscript to *Hunters in the Barrens*; namely, "how to protect these cultures from disintegration and at the same time help them to attain an effective bargaining position *vis-à-vis* the outside world wherein they can choose what they want, and reject what they do not want from the industrialized world" (p.120). While fully cognizant of the seductive influence of global, mass-consumer culture, Georg assisted the Innu in improving their bargaining position in various ways. These included the use of the written word and media interviews, playing inter-cultural, interpretative and advocacy roles in meetings with government representatives, and involvement in an environmental assessment panel for the Voisey's Bay nickel mining project.

I met Georg again in April 1991 in Davis Inlet where we both attended a political and cultural gathering organized by the Innu on the shores of a small, mainland lake called Natuashish ('Small Lake'). At the time, the provincial government of Clyde Wells was talking about investing considerable funds in water and sewage in Davis Inlet, a matter which Georg and I discussed with Chief Prote Poker in the basement of the old mission building. Concerns were raised there about the island village's limited physical capacity to support a growing Innu population and its attendant infrastructure.

In February the following year, a devastating house fire resulted in the death of six children and catapulted the Mushuau Innu into the media spotlight. The Innu quickly initiated a community inquiry to consider the reasons for the tragedy and examine solutions. Its findings were published and included a recommendation to relocate the community to an off-island location. Georg's good friend, Innu elder Kaniuekutat, stood firmly behind the recommendation: "We must let the government know that we want to move for better health, better living conditions, for water and sewage, so we can solve our community problems, so we can help our elders live more comfortably, and for better housing."[4]

---

3. See G. Henriksen. 1985. "Anthropologists as Advocates: Promoters of Pluralism or Makers of Clients?" in R. Paine (ed.), *Advocacy and Anthropology*. St. John's: ISER, pp.119–29
4. Innu Nation and Mushuau Innu Band Council. 1995. *Gathering Voices: Finding Strength to Help Our Children*. Vancouver: Douglas and McIntyre, p.133.

In January 1993, television images of gas-sniffing Innu youth in Davis Inlet reached international audiences and embarrassed the Canadian and Newfoundland governments into action to address Innu concerns and their call for relocation.[5] This is the context for Georg's 1993 visit to Davis Inlet where he was asked by the provincial government's Economic Recovery Commission to examine social and economic development options for the Mushuau Innu.[6] It was during that visit that Georg and Kaniuekutat began work on a project to record myths, as well as life-history and other narratives by Kaniuekutat, leading to the posthumous publication of Georg's book, *I Dreamed the Animals*, in 2009.[7]

A sequel of sorts to *Hunters in the Barrens*, *I Dreamed the Animals* is a loving tribute by Kaniuekutat to his tradition and pre-settlement life on the land, and a legacy to future generations of Innu. Framed by Georg's analysis of thirty-five years of profound social change since his first fieldwork experience among the Innu, and reflections on the lessons of Innu mythology, it gives voice to the preoccupations of Kaniuekutat and other Innu of his generation, who "clearly see and verbalise the dilemma in which they are caught: on the one hand they want the future generations of Innu to maintain Innu ways, their hunting skills and language and culture; on the other hand they see the necessity of learning English, mathematics and other skills that are crucial in the contemporary world."[8]

It is clear from Georg's closing chapter in *I Dreamed the Animals* that he considered the analysis first presented in *Hunters in the Barrens* to be relevant in the contemporary context, although he reframed the contrasting values of "sharing" versus "having," and "interdependence" versus "autonomy," in terms of a perennial Innu concern for their inclusion in or exclusion from the collectivity.[9] In the pre-settlement period, while living at interior caribou hunting camps, the Innu agreed upon the contexts in which their shared values of interdependence and sharing were relevant. These values were reinforced ritually and religiously through *makushan*,[10] respect for the animal

---

5. The Innu won their battle for relocation, and a new village was built at Natuashish. Resettlement began in December 2002.
6. G. Henriksen. 1993. 'Report on the Social and Economic Development of the Innu Community of Davis Inlet to the Economic Recovery Commission'. St. John's: Economic Recovery Commission.
7. G. Henriksen. 2009. *I Dreamed the Animals: Kaniuekutat, the Life of an Innu Hunter.* Oxford. Berghahn Books.
8. Henriksen, *I Dreamed the Animals*, p. 297.
9. See Henriksen, *I Dreamed the Animals*, p. 306.
10. Spelled *mokoshan* in the non-standard orthography.

masters and other means, and they bounded the continuous competition for prestige and leadership. In contrast, life in the village was characterized by an inability to "define unambiguously the situations or contexts in which particular values are agreed to be important and how they should circulate in relation to each other" (p.112). Furthermore, village life lacked the ritual means to collectively communicate shared values. Their growing involvement in a money-based economy and greatly enhanced opportunities to maximize personal autonomy through direct transactions with Euro-Canadian patrons precipitated the breakdown in sharing despite its importance in the maintenance of corporate values.

After settlement in Davis Inlet, Georg noted, frequent conflicts arose over economic transactions in which the sharing values of the Innu clashed with opportunities for individual possession and accumulation. Such conflicts arise in the new village of Natuashish as well, with heated and often bitter disputes over the allocation of new houses, the distribution of royalty revenues from the Voisey's Bay project,[11] employment through the band council and Innu Nation, and other scarce resources. Despite the overall increase in affluence compared to the pre-settlement period, these conflicts are, in my view, exacerbated by Innu interactions with more affluent neighbours and their status system, exposure to needs-stimulating mass marketing and the pernicious relative deprivation that results there from. A growing demand for industrially derived commodities imposes significant pressure on the Innu leadership and local economy to provide employment and income to meet the demand.

Furthermore, the redistributive mechanisms of the pre-settlement period no longer work, especially when it comes to goods and services unrelated to hunting. The animal masters have nothing to say about the redistribution of cash, iPods, video games, designer clothing and other commodities, and the ritual feast of *makushan* is no mechanism for the redistribution of new wealth obtained through lucrative band council jobs or joint venture businesses. The philosophy of progressive taxation – whereby the income of affluent elites is *shared* in order to finance community projects, services and other forms of common good – has never been seriously considered by the Innu, and in fact "tax" is a dirty word among them as it is among other Aboriginal people in Canada.

---

11. An Impact and Benefits Agreement signed between the Innu Nation and mining giant, Inco, in 2002 provided royalty payments, employment and business opportunities, co-management of social and environmental monitoring and mitigation measures, etc.

While caribou hunting continues to provide an important source of food to the Mushuau Innu, and is a high status pursuit, caribou no longer serve as the key resource in their competitive political relations, which focused in the pre-settlement period on the important role of the *utshimau*.[12] As Georg noted in *Hunters in the Barrens*, competition for this role and the prestige and followers associated with it made it difficult for the Innu to form corporate groups in the village context either for economic pursuits or political engagement with non-Innu and their institutions. Moreover, whereas the tutelage of non-Innu patrons such as the priest had limited, short-term effects in the pre-settlement period, life in the new village meant a rapidly increasing subjugation to the "welfare colonialism" of the Canadian nation-state with its "civilizing mission."[13]

Today, the new institutions of the band council and Innu Nation play a crucial role in countering that colonial grip, and demonstrate that the Mushuau Innu have been able to form corporate groups to deal with the outside world. Elected chiefs and councils have spearheaded demonstrations and hard-headed negotiations in an effort to obtain equitable terms for the exploitation of mineral and hydroelectric resources in their territory. They quickly became adept at the "politics of embarrassment" in their use of the news media in order to push governments to address their territorial rights and socio-economic needs. After all, the Canadian north suffers from a plethora of ravaged Aboriginal communities with social, health and economic problems of equivalent magnitude to those of the Mushuau Innu, yet their predicament attracts little attention from the media, the Canadian public and its governments. The success of the Mushuau Innu in winning their battle to relocate to Natuashish, negotiating an Impact and Benefits Agreement with Inco with respect to the Voisey's Bay mining project, and securing government support for healing and other programmes to deal with their social problems is a testimony to the political skill and determination of the Innu leadership as well as other community members.

Nonetheless, contemporary Innu leadership has many of the *utshimau* characteristics described by Georg in *Hunters in the Barrens*. The Innu remain ambivalent about leadership in that community members are dependent on the chief and council for access to employment and other scarce resources

---

12. Spelled *wotshimao* in the non-standard orthography, meaning 'one who takes the initiative in any given situation'.
13. See G. Henriksen. 1993. 'Life and Death Among the Mushuau Innu of Northern Labrador'. Research Paper 17. St. John's: ISER, p. 17.

that have commodity value within the broader global context. Their control over these resources is often resented by people who believe they are not getting their fair share, and that the benefits of office are distributed primarily through the close family networks of those in power to the exclusion of others. Obvious displays of wealth – that is, *having* more than other people – is politically dangerous for Innu leaders and invites great resentment.

Furthermore, leaders who are too aggressive in pushing healing programmes and other measures to deal with the social problems of the village may be accused of being "too *utshimau*"; that is, encroaching excessively on personal autonomy. For example, a referendum in 2008 in which the Mushuau Innu voted by a slim margin to ban alcohol was extremely unpopular with a drinking faction in the village, particularly since it was being enforced by the police. While airport luggage searches and arrests of "bootleggers" constitute serious infringements of personal autonomy, the chief supported such measures as the only viable way to curtail the tragically destructive effects of alcoholism. Thus, while an elected Innu leader now has access to "surpluses" that would facilitate binding other Innu to him as clients,[14] the leadership role continues to be precarious, as it is in many Aboriginal communities throughout Canada.

Georg's analysis in *Hunters in the Barrens* is a useful explanatory framework to make sense of contemporary Innu issues, "problematized" as they are by the media, and all too frequently reduced to negative stereotypes by non-Aboriginal people. Other academic analyses have advanced simplistic, victim theses that attribute Innu problems entirely to colonialism.[15] In contrast, Georg's analysis is nuanced and micro-processual and grants agency to the Innu themselves with respect to the efforts they make, or fail to make, to grapple with conflicting values, community factionalism, and the social pathologies of village life, all in the context of their encapsulation by the Canadian nation-state. While the collapse of Aboriginal communities elsewhere in Canada is often attributed to the "kidnapping" of children by the residential school system or land alienating events such as the invasion of immigrant agriculturalists, hydroelectric dams and pulp-wood extraction, foreign interference of such magnitude arrived tardily in Mushuau Innu

---

14. See Henriksen, 'Life and Death', p.19.
15. E.g., C. Samson. 2003. *A Way of Life That Does Not Exist: Canada and the Extinguishment of the Innu*. London, New York: Verso; cf. Georg's review of this book in *Newfoundland Studies*, 18, 2(2002): 316–21.

territory in the post-settlement period, and after myriad social pathologies had become well-entrenched. As a result, the root causes of Innu distress, complex as they are, must be explained by other means.

It is important to remember, however, that Georg never absolved Euro-Canadian governments and religious institutions of their responsibility in disempowering the Innu through various acts of tutelage, and he remained supportive of "counter-hegemonic" efforts by the Innu to pursue self-government and to control non-Innu interventions into their lives in the form of military flight training, mineral exploration and mining, hydroelectric development, and the unilateral imposition of foreign school and legal systems.

Georg admired the immense resiliency of the Mushuau Innu. He loved their wonderfully facetious humour and great generosity while at the same time empathizing with them when tragedy and sorrow struck. He had lived with them in the demanding Barren Ground environment of northern Labrador when they risked extreme cold and starvation and greatly respected their tenaciousness in the face of adversity. In the end, Georg remained optimistic that, provided with adequate resources and a legal-rights framework for the negotiation of their place in Canadian society, the Innu would achieve a healthy, proud and productive future for themselves.

Hunters in the Barrens is where Georg began his journey with the Mushuau Innu. It is an insightful guide for those searching for a path through the maze of confused and superficial public discourses concerning them, and for that reason it will be an enduring classic ethnography of Canadian Aboriginal peoples.

Peter Armitage,
St. John's, Newfoundland,
June 2009

Appendix

Figures 6 and 7 give the kinship terminology of the Naskapi. There are only two deviations from that given by Strong (1929). One is the term used for a man's sister's son and a woman's brother's son which are the same as for the children of ortho-siblings in the present terminology. However, the term given by Strong for children of hetero-siblings (*ntiwhotem*) is still known and sometimes used. The other deviation is the present practice of calling parallel-cousins *nihanes* instead of using the terms for siblings. However, the sibling terms are also used for this category.

The term *nihanes* can be translated as family. This term is also used by the Naskapi in Shefferville where Graburn (1965) reports that it is used for "those relatives who are excluded from sexual partnership by the rules of exogamy." With the same cross-cousin terminology as their relatives in Shefferville, it is more than likely that the Naskapi in Davis Inlet conceptualize the two categories of relatives by the same term. However, all my informants on the subject said that *nihanes* meant the same as *etatishenan,* or *eianesskats,* or *mishuemamo.* They said that all these terms referred to *all*

KEY to Kin Charts

A.	Napeo	M.	Ntihotem
B.	Niskwaw	N.	Notaon
C.	Nistish	O.	Nakaon
	Nishim	P.	Nohomesh
D.	Nemess	Q.	Nishokosh
	Nishim	R.	Ness
E.	Nistao	S.	Ntoss
F.	Nitomoss	T.	Nomoshoom
G.	Nihanes	U.	Nohom
H.	Nokoss	V.	Nowitshewage
I.	Ntanes	W.	Nossem
J.	Ntossem	X.	Nishim
K.	Ntossem Niskwim	Y.	Ntaneskooteban
L.	Naagen Niskwim		

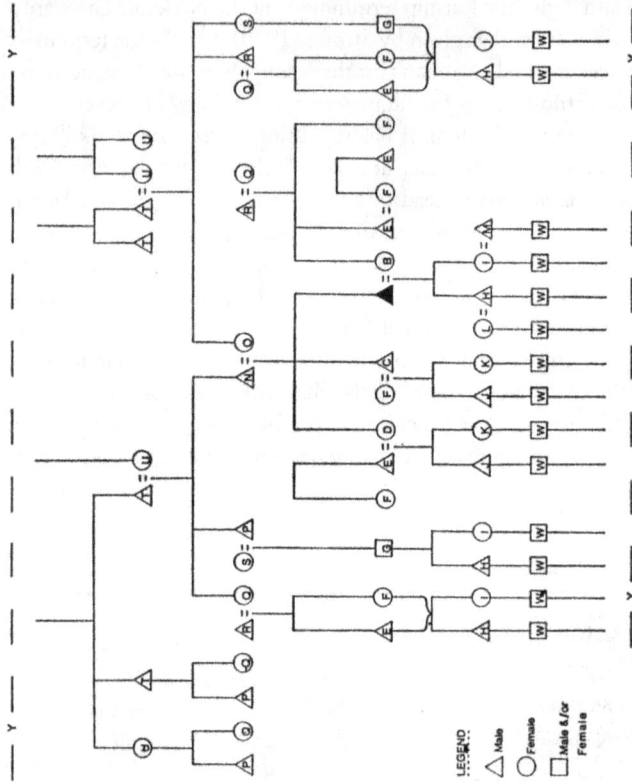

Figure 6. Naskapi Kinship Terminology

134

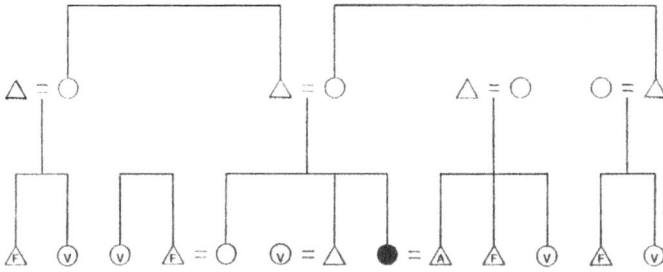

Figure 7. Naskapi Kinship Terminology (ego being female)

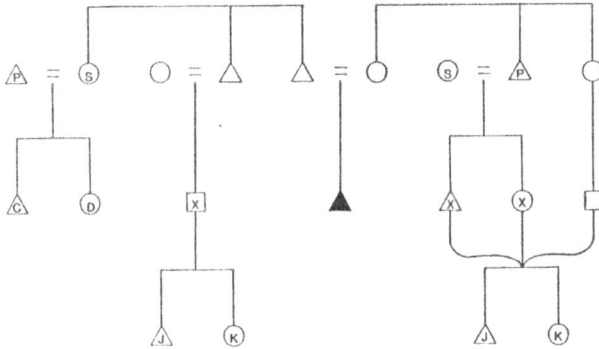

Figure 8. Naskapi Kinship Terminology Corresponding to Strong's (1929) for the Davis Inlet Band

relatives. I found no term by which they distinguish between relatives whom they can marry from those whom they are not allowed to marry.

Figure 8 gives the terminology that corresponds to Strong's for the Davis Inlet band. It was given to me by an old man, who is the only one, to my knowledge, to use it. Strong reports that out of fourteen marriages in the Barren Ground band, five were between cross-cousins, whereas there were no cross-cousin marriages in the neighbouring Davis Inlet band. He found a corresponding difference in the kinship terminology of the two bands, with that of the Barren Ground band being deeply influenced by the practice of cross-cousin marriage. Since Strong left Davis Inlet, the two bands merged into one around the mission and the trading post.

As far as I could determine, there are no cases of cross-cousin marriages among the Naskapi today. This is possibly because of the greater universe of marriageable partners resulting from the merging of the two bands, and also because of the influence of the Catholic Church which is against such marriages. During my stay in Davis Inlet, there were two cross-cousins who wanted to marry. However, the wedding was called off under pressure from the missionary. Although cross-cousin marriage is no longer practised, the Naskapi themselves still see it as permissible.

Since we find no cross-cousin marriages today, we can assume that the practice gradually disappeared. Therefore, the Davis Inlet band did *not* adopt the earlier practice of the Barren Ground band. However, the former Davis Inlet band adopted the kinship terminology of the Barren Ground band. The terminology has been retained by the former Barren Ground people, and almost universally adopted by the former Davis Inlet people.

There is only one informant who still uses the terminology of the Davis Inlet band as reported by Strong. He is the oldest male in Davis Inlet who, when he was about thirty, took Strong into the interior. In contrast to their father, his children have adopted the cross-cousin terminology.

Why the terminology changed in the direction it did, rather than in reverse is a matter of speculation. One factor may be the wish to have the possibility of marrying cross-cousins, whether it be for demographic reasons or for the excitement it entailed. Considering the Naskapi's tremendous preoccupation with love stories, the last suggestion might be plausible. Another possible factor behind the choice of the cross-cousin terminology may be that it designates roles that are more optimal in Naskapi social organization and ecological adaptation. Thus, the bonds between people designated by this terminology may be stronger and give one a greater option of whom one can affiliate with.

On the face of it, this is unlikely as the cross-cousin terminology has special terms for cross-cousins (*nistao* and *nitomoss*), whereas the terminology of the former Davis Inlet band has the same terms for cross-cousins and for siblings. Thus, one would think that the bonds designated between cross-cousins in this system were more intimate and easily activated than those designated by the cross-cousin terminology. This, however, is not necessarily so: first, because the bonds between brothers are not particularly strong, and secondly, because the relationship between people of the same sex who call each other *nistao* or *nowitshewage* (man and woman, respectively) are filled with warmth and affection. This relationship is extended to cross-cousins in the ideology of the cross-cousin terminology. Furthermore, the relationship between hetero-cross-cousins is socially enhanced by the fact that they are potential spouses and engage in sexual "horseplay." Another indication of the importance for the Naskapi of embracing as many people as possible by extending their kinship network, is their practice of sponsorship at baptisms. Thus, godparents call their godchildren daughters and sons, and the godchildren call their godparents mother and father. The godchildren and the children of the godparents call each other brother and sister.

References

BALIKCI, A.
1968 "Bad Friend." *Human Organization,* 27(3).

BARTH, F.(ed.)
1963 *The Role of the Entrepreneur in Social Change in Northern Norway.* Oslo, Universitetsforlaget.

BARTH, F.
1964 *Nomads of South Persia, the Basseri Tribe of the Khamseh Confederacy.* New York, Humanities Press.

BARTH, F.
1966 *Models of Social Organization.* Royal Anthropological Institute Occasional Paper, 23. London.

BEN-DOR, S.
1966 *Makkovik: Eskimos and Settlers in a Labrador Community.* St. John's, Institute of Social and Economic Research, Memorial University of Newfoundland.

BLEHR, O.
1963 "Action Groups in a Society with Bilateral Kinship: A Case Study from the Faroe Islands." *Ethnology,* 2(3).

DAMAS, D. (ed.)
1969a *Contributions to Anthropology: Band Societies.* National Museum of Canada, Bulletin No. 228. Ottawa, Queen's Printer.

DAMAS, D. (ed.)
1969b *Contributions to Anthropology: Ecological Essays.* National Museum of Canada, Bulletin No. 230. Ottawa, Queen's Printer.

DAVIES, K.G. (ed.)
1963 *Northern Quebec and Labrador Journals and Correspondence 1819-35.* London, Hudson's Bay Record Society.

DUNNING, R.W.
1959 "Ethnic Relations and the Marginal Man in Canada." *Human Organization,* 18(3).

DURKHEIM, E.
1965 *The Elementary Forms of the Religious Life.* New York, The Free Press.

GOFFMAN, E.
1967 *Interaction Ritual: Essays on Face-to-Face Behavior.* New York, Doubleday & Company, Inc.

GRABURN, N.H.H.
1965 "Cross-Cousin Marriage and the Naskapi." Paper read at the annual meetings of the American Anthropological Association in Denver.

GUEMPLE, D.L.

1970 "Eskimo, Bands and the 'D P Camp' Hypothesis." Preliminary draft, St. John's, Institute of Social and Economic Research, Memorial University of Newfoundland.

HAWTHORNE, H.B. (ed.)

1966 *A Survey of the Contemporary Indians of Canada.* Indian Affairs Branch, Ottawa.

HELM, J.

1961 *The Lynx Point People: The Dynamics of a Northern Athapaskan Band.* National Museum of Canada, Bulletin No. 176. Ottawa, Department of Northern Affairs and National Resources.

HENRIKSEN, G.

1971 "The Transactional Basis of Influence: White Men among Naskapi Indians." In R. Paine (ed.), *Patrons and Brokers in the East Arctic.* St. John's, Institute of Social & Economic Research, Memorial University of Newfoundland.

HILLER, J.

1971 "Early Patrons of the Labrador Eskimos: The Moravian Mission in Labrador, 1764–1805." In R. Paine (ed.), *Patrons and Brokers in the East Arctic.* St. John's, Institute of Social & Economic Research, Memorial University of Newfoundland.

HONIGMANN, J.J.

1949 *Culture and Ethos of Kaska Society.* Yale University Publications in Anthropology, No. 40. New Haven, Yale University Press.

HONIGMANN, J.J.

1962 *Social Networks in Great Whale River; Notes on an Eskimo Montagnai-Naskapi, and Euro-Canadian Community.* National Museum of Canada, Bulletin No. 178. Ottawa, Department of Northern Affairs and National Resources.

HONIGMANN, J.J.

1968 "Interpersonal Relations in Atomistic Communities." *Human Organization,* 27(3).

JENNESS, D.

1965 *Eskimo Administration: III Labrador.* Montreal, Arctic Institute of North America, Technical Paper No. 16.

KLEIVAN, H.

1966 *The Eskimos of Northeast Labrador; A History of Eskimo-White Relations, 1771–1955.* Oslo, Norsk Polarinstitutt, Skrifter Nr. 139.

KNIGHT, R.

1965 "A Re-examination of Hunting, Trapping and Territoriality among the Northeastern Algonkian Indians." In A. Leeds & A.P. Vayda (eds), *Man, Culture and Animals; the Role of Animals in Human Ecological Adjustments.* Washington, American Association for the Advancement of Science.

LEACH, E.R.
1954 *Political Systems of Highland Burma; A Study of Kachin Social Structure.* Cambridge, Harvard University Press.

LEACOCK, E.
1954 *The Montagnais Hunting Territory and the Fur Trade.* American Anthropological Association, Memoir No. 78.

LEACOCK, E.
1955 "Matrilocality in a Simple Hunting Economy (Montagnais-Naskapi)." *Southwestern Journal of Anthropology,* 11:31–47.

LEACOCK, E.
1969 "The Montagnais-Naskapi Band." In D. Damas (ed.), *Contributions to Anthropology: Band Societies.* National Museum of Canada, Bulletin No. 228.

MILLS, C.W.
1959 *The Sociological Imagination.* New York, Oxford University Press.

MOORE, O.K.
1965 "Divination – A New Perspective." *American Anthropologist,* 59.

MURPHY, R.F., and J.H. STEWARD
1956 "Tappers and Trappers: Parallel Process in Acculturation." *Economic Development and Cultural Change,* 4.

PAINE, R.
1969 "In Search of Friendship: An Exploratory Analysis in 'Middle-class' Culture." *Man,* 4(4).

PAINE, R. (ed.)
1971 *Patrons and Brokers in the East Arctic.* St. John's, Institute of Social & Economic Research, Memorial University of Newfoundland.

PARK, G.K.
1963 "Divination and its Social Contexts." *The Journal of the Royal Anthropological Institute of Great Britain and Ireland,* Vol. 93, Part 2.

POLANYI, K., ARENSBERG, C. M., and H.W. PEARSON
1957 *Trade and Market in the Early Empires; Economies in History and Theory.* Glencoe, Ill., The Free Press.

RIDINGTON, W.R.
1968 "The Environmental Context of Beaver Indian Behavior." Ph.D. Thesis, Harvard University.

ROBBINS, R.H.
1968 "Role Reinforcement and Ritual Deprivation: Drinking Behaviour in a Naskapi Village." Paper read at the 8th Annual Meeting of the Northeastern Anthropological Association, Dartmouth College, N.H.

ROGERS, E.S.
1962 *The Round Lake Ojibwa.* University of Toronto, Royal Ontario Museum, Art and Archeology Division, Occasional Paper 5.

ROGERS, E.S.
1969 "Band Organization Among the Indians of Eastern Subarctic Canada." In D. Damas (ed.), *Contributions to Anthropology: Band Societies.* National Museum of Canada, Bulletin No. 228.

SAHLINS, M.
  1965 "On the Sociology of Primitive Exchange." In M. Banton (ed.), *The Relevance of Models for Social Anthropology,* ASA Monographs No. 1. London, Tavistock.
SCHUMACHER, E.F.
  1970 "The Economics of Permanence." *Resurgence,* 3(1).
SERVICE, E.
  1962 *Primitive Social Organization, an Evolutionary Perspective.* New York, Random House.
SPECK, F. G.
  1935 *Naskapi, The Savage Hunters of the Labrador Peninsula.* Norman, University of Oklahoma Press.
SPECK, F.G., and LOREN C. EISELEY
  1939 "The Significance of the Hunting Territory Systems of the Algonkian in Social Theory." *American Anthropologist,* 41.
SPECK, F.G., and LOREN C. EISELEY
  1942 "Montagnais-Naskapi Bands and Family Hunting Districts of the Central and Southern Labrador Peninsula." Proceedings of the American Philosophical Society, 85.
STRONG, W. D.
  1929 "Cross-Cousin Marriage and the Culture of the North-eastern Algonkian." *American Anthropologist,* 31.
TANNER, V.
  1944 *Outlines of the Geography, Life and Customs of Newfoundland-Labrador.* Helsinki, Acta Geographica, 8.
THWAITES, R.G. (ed.)
  1906 *The Jesuit Relations and Allied Documents.* Cleveland, Burrow Bros. Co.
TURNER, L.M.
  1887 "On the Indians and Eskimos of the Ungava District, Labrador." Canada, *Royal Society Proceedings and Transactions,* 5(2).
WILLIAMS, G.
  1963 "Introduction." In K.G. Davies (ed.), *Northern Quebec and Labrador Journals and Correspondence, 1819–35.* London, Hudson's Bay Record Society.

Index

www.ingramcontent.com/pod-product-compliance
Lightning Source LLC
Chambersburg PA
CBHW072132020426
42334CB00018B/1765